PATCHWORK
QUILTING AND
APPLIQUÉ

ACKNOWLEDGEMENTS

We sincerely appreciate the talents and hard work of the following quilters:
Pippa Abrahams p103, Pat Allen p149, Deirdre Amsden p107, C June Barnes p163,
Peggy Bell pp73 and 81, Ngaire Brooks p103, Jill Cawrey p108, Susan Chastney p115,
Sally Connor p166, Janice Cook p153, Jo Davey p134, Maggie Davies p143,
Sue Day p149, Dilys Fronks p141, Judith Gill p63, Katharine Guerrier p83,
Jan Hale p114, Carole Hart p165, Yoko Hatcher p164, Yvonne Holland p32,
Annlee Landman p105, Irene MacWilliam p115, Makower & Co, Ltd for supplying
the fabrics featured in the Flying Geese Lap Quilt on p55, Linda Maltman pp45 and 159,
Rosemary Muntus kindly loaned the sashiko quilting featured on p164,
Dolly Parker p79, Patricia Payn p137, Sheila Pearson p149, Maria Reuter pp111 and 117,
Brian Smith kindly loaned the Antique Crazy quilt featured on p89, Veronika Smith pp55
and 61, Elizabeth Snodgrass p99, Rosalind Sutton p129,
Gisela Thwaites pp91 and 158, Anne Tuck p146, June Walters p32
Many thanks to Angela Guppy, Mary Mayne, Irene Nowell, Helen Raine,
Rowena Reamonn, and Gill Tanner for their support.

A READER'S DIGEST BOOK
Published by The Reader's Digest Association Limited
11 Westferry Circus, Canary Wharf, London E14 4HE

Conceived, edited and designed by
MQ Publications, 254–258 Goswell Road, London EC1V 7EB

Copyright © 1998 MQ Publications Ltd

ISBN 0 276 42346 1

A CIP data record for this book is available from the British Library.

Editor: Ljiljana Ortolja-Baird
Illustrator: Penny Brown
Designer: Bet Ayer
Technical reader: Vivien Finch
Photography: Graham Seager and Stewart Grant

Printed and bound in Italy

PATCHWORK QUILTING AND APPLIQUÉ

THE COMPLETE GUIDE TO ALL THE ESSENTIAL TECHNIQUES

JENNI DOBSON

Reader's Digest

LONDON • NEW YORK • SYDNEY • CAPE TOWN • MONTREAL

Contents

....

APPLIQUÉ · 118–153

QUILTING · 154–165

FINISHING · 166–173

TEMPLATES · 174–191

INDEX · 192

BASIC SKILLS

Basic Skills offers all the essential definitions, skills and techniques needed for quilt making. Whether you wish to sew by hand or by machine, you will find simple instructions to cover all approaches to choosing equipment, cutting, piecing, appliqué, pressing, quilt assembly and layering, quilting and finishing.

Working through the key stages set out in this section is just like taking a series of classes with a teacher. By the end of the section, you will be familiar with commonly used quilting terms and the processes that they describe. This methodical approach will enable you to take on any of the techniques described in later sections of the book.

Try to do each stage as well as possible, but do not be too critical – it is better to experience the pleasure of completing a project and feeling motivated to start another than to set such high standards for yourself that you never finish anything.

The first project, *Hearts and Hourglasses,* has been designed to put all the basics into practice as well as offer scope for individual interpretation. It will give a beginner sufficient expertise to undertake any future quilt project with confidence.

Left: Detail of nineteenth-century *Four-patch* quilt

Getting to Know Your Quilt

....

A quilt is made up of three layers of fabric. A decorative top, a middle lining and a backing are known as the quilt 'sandwich'. The layers are held together with a decorative running stitch (the quilting) or by a simpler method of tying.

1 QUILT TOP
The upper layer of the quilt sandwich. The top can be pieced, appliquéd or cut as a single piece of fabric.

2 WADDING
The middle layer, or the 'filling' in a quilt. It can be made of cotton, wool, silk, or synthetic fibres *(see page 16)*.

3 BACKING
The bottom layer of the quilt sandwich *(see pages 15 and 170)*.

4 BLOCK
A single design unit that when sewn together with other blocks creates the quilt top. A block is most often a square, hexagon, or rectangle, but it can be any shape. It can be pieced, plain, or appliquéd.

5 PIECED BLOCK
A single design unit made up of several smaller units or pieces.

6 ALTERNATE BLOCK
A plain square used in the design to contrast and alternate with pieced or appliquéd blocks.

7 SASHING/SETTING STRIPS
Strips of fabric used to join blocks.

8 SETTING SQUARE/POST
A square of fabric that joins sashing to sashing at the intersection of the component blocks.

9 ON-POINT BLOCK
A block turned on its corner to read as a diamond.

10 CORNER TRIANGLE
A triangle cut with the straight grain around the right-angle corner and used to square up blocks on-point.

11 SETTING TRIANGLE
A triangle with the straight grain down the long side and used to fill-in between blocks on-point.

12 APPLIQUÉ BLOCK
A block made by sewing fabric shapes onto a background, either by hand or by machine. Usually representational.

13 FRAMING STRIPS
Narrow strips of fabric sewn around all four sides of a block like a picture frame. They function to clarify the design, enlarge blocks, and stabilise the edges of a complex piecing design.

14 INNER BORDER
An internal frame of fabric designed to draw together the various central design motifs. This device is often used with pieced outer borders.

15 MITRED CORNER
A corner finished by sewing the fabric strips at a 45° angle *(see page 168)*.

16 BUTTED CORNER
A corner finished by sewing strips at right angles *(see page 168)*.

17 OUTER BORDER
A frame of fabric strips sewn to the sides of the quilt top. Borders can be narrow, wide, pieced, plain or appliquéd. They unify the overall design and draw attention to the central area *(see page 168)*.

18 PIECED BORDER
A border made up of various fabric pieces that gives the quilt a more decorative finish.

19 APPLIQUÉ BORDER
Often used as a decorative complement to an appliquéd quilt top.

20 CORNER BLOCK OR POST
A square that joins the horizontal and vertical border strips.

21 ROUNDED CORNER
An alternative to square corners that requires a bias binding. Selective cutting of striped fabric draws the eye to the corner.

22 QUILTING
A decorative running stitch sewn by hand or machine that holds the three layers of the quilt together *(see page 155)*.

23 BINDING
A narrow fabric strip used to finish the raw edges of a quilt *(see page 171)*.

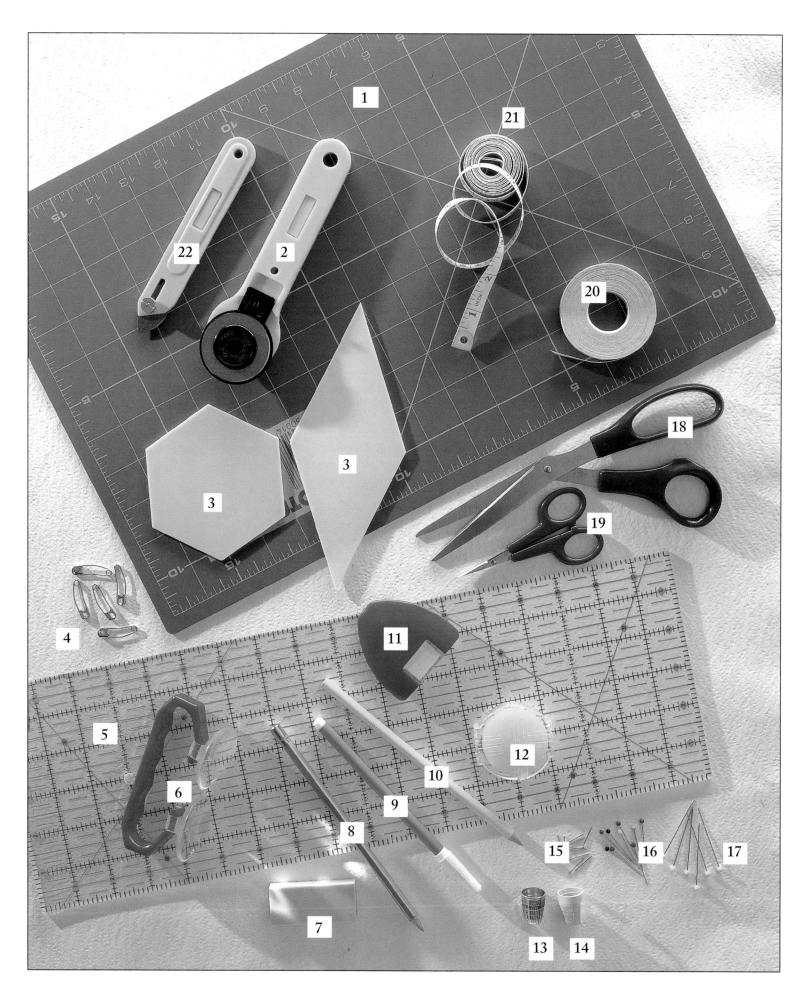

Equipment and Supplies

· ·

It is helpful to remember that quilts can be made with the simplest of tools. In the past, magnificent quilts were made using only needles, pins, scissors, pencil and a ruler. There are lots of tempting goodies available at quilting supply stores; part of your progression from beginner to experienced quilt maker will include discovering which of those are most useful. As a rule, buy the best tools you can afford.

EQUIPMENT

A basic list that you will find useful for making quilts. The list corresponds to the numbered items on page 10.

1 · Self-healing Cutting Mat
2 · Rotary Cutter (large)
3 · Plastic Templates
4 · Safety Pins
5 · Plastic Cutting Ruler
6 · Rubber or Plastic Template Suction Handle
7 · Fabric Eraser
8 · Silver Marking Pencil
9 · Cold-water-soluble Marker
10 · Yellow Marking Pencil
11 · Chalk Holder
12 · Beeswax in Holder
13 · Metal Thimble
14 · Plastic Open-ended Thimble
15 · Sequin Pins
16 · Ball-headed Pins
17 · Extra-long Pins
18 · Fabric Shears
19 · Embroidery Scissors
20 · Masking Tape (2.5 cm width)
21 · Tape Measure
22 · Craft Knife

SEWING MACHINE

Although many quilters enjoy handwork, most would agree that a sewing machine is high on the equipment list.

Determine which functions you need most and choose a machine accordingly. It is not necessary to have the most expensive model to produce good work. Computerised machines may take longer to use efficiently and can be more costly to repair if anything goes wrong.

Talk to the sales assistants and buy from a supplier willing to offer support and service. Ask to read the machine manual to see how easy it is to follow. Enquire whether classes are available to help you get the most out of your machine. Find out if extra fittings and attachments, such as darning or walking (even-feed) feet, are available and what each one costs.

For travelling to classes, portability and the weight of your machine should be taken into consideration.

Using Your Sewing Machine

1 Check that the machine is clean and put in a new needle for each new project. A size 80/12 needle is suitable for most quilt-making tasks.

2 Thread your machine with the same weight thread for the needle and bobbin. To save time when sewing large projects, wind two bobbins.

3 Check the tension for each project by sewing together two fabrics from the project. The top thread and the lower thread should lock together between the two fabric layers.

If the needle thread is pulled through to the lower side, this means the top tension is too loose.

If the bobbin thread is pulled to the top of the work, then the needle (or top) tension is too tight.

Check the overall appearance of the seam. Again, if the fabric puckers, the tension is too tight.

4 Care for your machine as directed in the manual. Note that some computerised machines can only be professionally serviced. Keep all magnetic items well away from computerised machines.

5 Take care to remove all fragments when a needle is broken. Dispose of damaged or broken needles safely.

NEEDLES

Needles are sold in packets of mixed sizes or all of one size. For a beginner, mixed packets are most useful. Experiment with different sizes on various fabrics to discover what works best.

For hand piecing, hand appliqué and finishing bindings, use 'sharps'. They are moderately long, with some flexibility and an easy-to-thread eye. For exceptionally fine work, some quilters like to use embroidery or crewel needles.

Use 'betweens' for quilting. They are shorter and have less flexibility. If you are a beginner, start with a larger-size needle and progress to a smaller one as you gain experience.

Large, long needles such as darning needles, 'straws', and even doll-making needles, are useful for basting the quilt layers together.

PINS

Buy good-quality pins. Do not use burred or rusted pins or pins from packaging as they will mark your fabric.

Use long pins with ball or plastic heads rather than dressmaker's pins. They are easier to push through the fabric.

Extra-long pins are available for assembling the quilt layers. Safety pins (size 2) can be used for basting.

For appliqué, use 1.5 cm or 2 cm sequin pins to hold little shapes in place.

THIMBLES

Many quilters sew successfully without a thimble, but learning to use one will definitely reduce the likelihood of sore fingers while quilting. A thimble should fit snugly on the finger that you use to push the needle through the fabric. To help keep the thimble on, moisten your fingertip before putting it on. A good tip for beginners is to wear the thimble continuously until it feels like a 'second skin'.

Thimbles come in metal, plastic, wood or leather and include the open-ended type, with which the user pushes the needle with the side of the finger. Others have a slight ridge around the top to prevent the needle from slipping off the end.

There are thimble substitutes, such as tape or patches of plastic, for those who cannot keep a conventional thimble on their finger.

SCISSORS

A good pair of sharp dressmaker's shears is essential for cutting fabrics accurately and should be reserved for cutting fabric only. When choosing scissors, always test the balance and try them for comfort. Poorly balanced or uncomfortable scissors will make your hands ache very quickly.

Have another pair of scissors for cutting paper and plastic templates.

Use a pair of small embroidery scissors with very sharp points for fine appliqué work, trimming threads, and clipping seam allowances.

Specialist scissors are available for reverse appliqué.

TEMPLATE-MAKING EQUIPMENT

To make templates you will need cardboard or template plastic, a pencil or fine marker, and a ruler or straightedge. Use template plastic rather than cardboard if the template will be used repeatedly.

To cut the shapes, use scissors or an craft knife, which gives more precise results. Always use your craft knife with a metal-edge ruler.

To draft original designs, you may need a set square and a compass.

ROTARY CUTTING EQUIPMENT

For quick and accurate cutting, use a rotary cutter along with a self-healing cutting mat and a thick plastic, see-through ruler. Large cutters can slice through up to eight layers of fabric; smaller ones are useful for cutting curves and small pieces. All cutters are fitted with a safety guard because the blades are very sharp.

Never use the cutter on any surface other than a self-healing mat, as anything else will quickly blunt the blade. Cutting mats come in various sizes. A large mat allows you to cut much larger pieces of fabric and removes the need to handle and fold the fabric as often. Small mats are ideal for transporting to classes. Many quilters find that owning more than one mat is the answer. Mats are generally marked with a grid to help cut bigger pieces of fabric and for lining up the edges of the fabric.

Use a heavy-duty, see-through plastic ruler with your rotary cutter. Choose either a 16 x 60 cm or 10 x 45 cm ruler that is marked in centimetres, 0.5 cm and 0.25 cm and 30°, 45° and 60° angles. Before buying a ruler, place it over assorted printed fabrics to check that the measurements can be read easily.

In addition to basic rulers, there is also a wide variety of rulers for cutting specific shapes, which are, in effect, like multi-size templates. Often, these are designed for a particular piecing technique.

IRON

Pressing is essential to accurate piecing, and your iron and ironing board should be kept close to your work. Use a steam iron because the steam will help set seams.

Travel irons are popular for classes, and they can be set up right beside your sewing machine for easy pressing between stages.

A small ironing pad or fabric board wrapped in a towel can serve as a portable pressing surface.

MARKING EQUIPMENT

For marking seam allowances, tracing around templates, or marking a quilting design, always use a non-permanent marker. An ordinary well-sharpened graphite pencil is suitable for marking most fabrics. For dark fabrics, on which pencil marks cannot easily be read, use coloured, air-, or water-soluble markers, a chalk wheel, a sharpened sliver of hard-dried soap or a pencil with white or silver-grey lead.

If you prefer not to 'draw' on your quilt top, other marking methods include masking tape (for geometric designs only), adhesive plastic templates, or a hera marker, a Japanese marking tool that lightly scores the design onto the fabric.

Use permanent markers only for writing quilt labels or drawing in details on appliqué.

Unwanted pencil marks can be removed without damaging the fabric with a special fabric eraser.

YARDSTICK

Use a yardstick with a triangle to straighten the edges of each of your fabric pieces.

MEASURING TAPE

Use a 300 cm quilt maker's tape rather than the regular dressmaker's tape, which measures 150 cm long.

THREAD

Always use good-quality thread for all your work. A 100 percent cotton or cotton-covered polyester is most suitable for hand and machine piecing and appliqué. Choose a colour that matches your fabric. Only use dark thread when sewing dark fabrics because any ends of dark thread will show through adjacent lighter fabrics in the finished quilt. When sewing different colours and patterns together, choose a medium to light neutral thread, such as grey or ecru. As an alternative, use 'invisible', or monofilament, nylon thread.

For both machine and hand quilting, use a coated or pre-waxed quilting thread. It is stronger than regular sewing thread, and the coating allows it to glide through the quilt layers. If you use regular sewing cotton for quilting, try running your thread lightly across some beeswax.

Hand quilting can be worked with other special threads, such as pearl or crochet cotton.

For tying, use embroidery thread, pearl cotton or crochet cotton.

For basting, choose a light-coloured thread. If you decide to use an inferior-quality basting thread, tiny fibres may shed when the thread is pulled through the fabric.

Store your spools in a dust-proof container away from direct sunlight.

SPECIALIST EQUIPMENT

Bias Bars Re-usable metal strips useful when long lengths of bias strips of a consistent appearance are needed – for instance, when working stained-glass appliqué or Celtic designs.

Creative Grid 115 cm-wide flannel printed with a 5 cm grid mounted on a wall or foam board makes an ideal design wall.

Hot Pen Device for cutting template shapes from durable plastic.

Cut-and-press Board A rotary cutting mat on one side and a padded pressing surface on the other. These are available in several sizes.

Multisize Plastic Templates Suitable for use with a rotary cutter, these templates allow you to cut many different sizes of one specific shape.

Quick Stripper Adjustable cutter that slices two sets of strips, from 2.5–15 cm wide, at once.

Rotary Blade Sharpener Easy appliance to use for restoring the edge of the cutter blade.

Specialist Rulers These rulers, intended for use with more challenging designs, such as wedges and logs for pineapple patterns, are a timesaving device for all quilters.

Stencil Cutting Knife This knife is useful for cutting templates and parallel channels in quilting stencils.

Fabric and Colour

....

Fabric is the heart of quilt making, and manipulating its colour and pattern is one of the great joys of patchwork. Once bitten by the quilting bug, quilt makers become compulsive purchasers of fabric, and having a beautiful collection that includes all the colours of the rainbow is almost as pleasurable as finishing their first quilt.

Often, the basic colour for a quilt is pre-determined; it is choosing the colours to go with it that causes quilters the most anxiety. A design worked with different fabrics can yield distinctly different results. A fascinating exercise is to make up the same block using a variety of different fabrics and to observe how the placement of colour and pattern can affect the block's final appearance. It is

important to choose fabrics that harmonise without becoming bland. Choose colours and patterns you like and will enjoy working with. Your fabric collection will grow with each quilt you make, and you should aim to put together a complete palette of colours and values (*value* is the degree of lightness or darkness of a colour). Having a good selection of fabrics from across the colour spectrum allows you to make more interesting choices. Sometimes small amounts of the most unlikely colour or colour value enhance an otherwise predictable scheme.

By arranging your colour values in a certain way you can make some areas of your quilt recede and others advance. Light colours seem to advance and attract attention while

dark colours appear to recede. This principle is important if you want to highlight certain areas of your quilt. The clever placement of light, medium and dark values can create optical illusions.

In your quilts, you will use a variety of prints (patterned fabrics) and solid-colour fabrics, also called plains. Use a combination of small-, medium- and large-scale prints in your work. Remember that small-scale prints will appear, or read, solid from a distance. However, they are often a more interesting choice than a plain solid colour.

Below: Detail of nineteenth-century *Tumbling Blocks* quilt pieced in solid colours of light, medium and dark values, which give the quilt its three-dimensional effect.

For piecing and appliqué, use 100 percent cotton fabrics. Cotton handles well and will take a crease; thus, it suits appliqué, and it presses well for piecing. Not all fabrics labelled '100 percent cotton' are the same, and not all are right for quilt making.

Cotton can include knits, corduroy, upholstery fabrics, broderie anglaise and sailcloth. Fabrics like these, especially knits, are best avoided by the beginners although sometimes they suit the inspirations of a more experienced quilter.

Look at the weave of the fabric – a loose-weave fabric allows the wadding to escape, and tightly woven fabrics are difficult to hand quilt. Dress-weight cottons are best for beginners. If an upholstery fabric appeals to you but you are unsure about whether you should use it, imagine wearing a blouse made with it. If you think it would be comfortable, then it is probably appropriate for your quilt.

Polyester-cotton blends can be used for piecing, provided they are more than 50 percent cotton. They are not suitable for hand appliqué, as they do not stay turned under long enough to be stitched into place. They are better used as backgrounds for appliqué. Beware when pressing: an iron hot enough to press the cotton pieces may shrink the blended fabrics slightly.

Some techniques require special fabrics. Crazy patchwork uses velvets, brocades, satins and silks. Sheer organdy is used for shadow appliqué. Silk is a favourite of experienced quilters, although is not recommended for a beginner's first project.

If you decide to recycle fabrics, make sure that they are not too distressed, or you will find yourself having to repair or replace worn patches after the quilt is finished.

Wherever possible, use fabrics of similar weight and type in one project.

BUYING FABRIC

Fabrics come in a variety of different widths. The most readily available is 112–115 cm wide, and most of the fabric requirements listed in our projects are based on this width.

There is a good range of solid colours available in 150 cm-wide fabrics. A few speciality fabrics, such as Liberty's Tana lawn, are produced only in 90 cm widths.

Calico is often used for backing quilts, backgrounds of blocks and home-dyeing. It is available in a range of widths, from 90 to 275 cm. This diversity makes it a more practical choice for backing quilts of any size because you can simply buy the width that best fits the project in hand.

Buying fat quarters of a metre (50 cm long x 56 cm wide) is a very convenient way to buy small amounts of many fabrics. The cut is made by dividing a metre of 112–115 cm-wide fabric in half both vertically and horizontally. Often, a fat quarter is a more useful shape than the conventional 0.25 metre cut (long quarter), which yields a piece 25 cm long x 112–115 cm wide. However, for a project requiring a few long, narrow strips, the latter would be more suitable. Although many quilting stores sell fat quarters, be aware that some sell fabric only in conventional cuts.

SELVAGE AND GRAIN

The selvage is the tightly woven edge of the fabric and should be trimmed before cutting.

The grain is the direction of the threads in woven fabric. The lengthwise grain (warp) runs parallel to the selvage and has very little stretch. The crosswise grain (weft) runs at right angles to the selvage and is slightly stretchy. The diagonal direction is the bias. It has the most stretch, making it ideal for bindings.

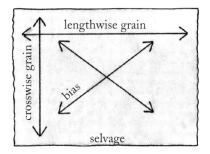

Whenever possible, place the weft and the warp parallel to the outer edges of the block. Always mark the grain lines on templates and pattern pieces.

PREPARING FABRIC

Pre-wash new fabrics before storing. This should be done immediately after purchase. Washing removes the sizing (making the fabric easier to work with) as well as any excess dye. Sort your fabrics into darks, mediums, and lights. Wash separately in warm water, with a tiny amount of mild soap. It is not unusual to notice some traces of colour in the water. This colour would not normally transfer onto other fabrics when sewn into a quilt. However, if a fabric sheds a lot of dye in the rinse it is probably not colour-fast and further washing is advisable. Alternatively, soak the fabric for a few hours in a solution of one part salt or vinegar to three parts water.

After washing, when the fabric is almost dry, straighten the grain if necessary. Do this by first pulling the fabric diagonally across in both directions and then again in the direction in which it appears short. Bring the selvages together and press very lightly down the length of the fabric. Fold the fabric neatly and allow to dry completely before storing.

WADDING

In the past, quilt fillings have included lambswool, blankets, worn quilts, or whatever was on hand. Recent years have seen a tremendous increase in the variety of wadding available. Wadding is described by its fibre content and weight. All commercially available wadding must conform to minimum flame retardancy regulations. This means not that it will not burn but that it will not burn faster than a pre-determined rate. The most widely used fibre for wadding is polyester. Its stability means the quilting lines can be stitched further apart without fear of the wadding shifting. Polyester also extends the life of a quilt. Cotton, wool, or silk waddings often contain a percentage of the fibre for this reason.

Some battings with a high proportion of cotton will shrink when washed. Pre-wash these varieties before sewing. If you intend giving your quilt an 'antique' appearance, use a cotton wadding but do not pre-wash it. The wadding will shrink causing the quilt top to wrinkle.

Whether you plan to hand or machine quilt will affect the choice of wadding used. Wadding is often described in terms of its weight, such as 25 gm or 50 gm, but it can be compressed in the manufacturing process so that the same weight appears thinner. This is known as low-loft wadding and is very good for machine quilting. Thick and fluffy wadding is called high-loft and is a popular filling for comforters, children's quilts or tied projects.

For wall hangings and clothing, use needlepunched wadding. It is very stable and hangs well.

Wadding is sold off the roll in various widths and also in pre-cut pieces suitable for all bed-size quilts.

Natural-fibre wadding comes in white or off-white, but a charcoal-coloured version is available for use with quilt tops of mainly dark colours.

Occasionally, tiny fibres from the batting work their way through to the top and create a hazy coating over the surface. This process is called 'bearding' and is more noticeable on dark fabrics. If bearding happens, lightly 'shave' the surface with a razor – do not pull the fibres out.

Store wadding with as few folds as possible. A day or two before you plan to use it, spread it out to encourage any creases to fall out.

ESTIMATING QUANTITY

Although our projects list quantities, it is useful to be able to estimate quantity requirements. A simple method is to make a drawing on graph paper that represents a few metres of 112–115 cm-wide fabric. Onto this plan, you mark the amounts required for each fabric in turn. Indicate the quantity in pencil so that each calculation can be erased and the plan used many times over.

1 Mark the length with 25-cm divisions.

2 For example, to work out the quantity for 20 squares, each 20 cm (cut size), mark a strip 20 cm across the width of the fabric, then mark off 20 cm squares. The illustration shows that you will get five squares from one strip. Therefore, you will need four strips (each 20 cm wide), giving a total length of 80 cm, to yield 20 squares, each 20 cm.

3 Always round up to the next 10 cm because the fabric may need to be straightened; it is also wise to have a little extra in case a piece has to be recut.

4 If you need pieces of a different size in the same fabric, repeat the process with the new size. It is sensible to begin with the largest piece. Sometimes, smaller pieces can be cut from trimmings.

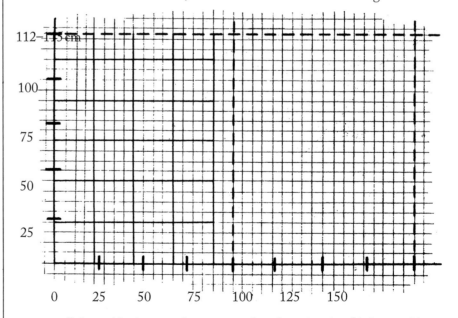

Enlarge this plan to make your own chart for estimating fabric quantities

Converting to Imperial

....

METRIC TO IMPERIAL CONVERSIONS

FABRIC QUANTITIES

A yard is smaller than a metre by 8.6 cm. To ensure you have enough cloth when converting to imperial, add ⅛ yard extra for every part yard. For amounts below 1 metre buy ⅛ yard more than the numerical equivalent.

Metre	Yard
1	1⅛
1.2	1⅜
1.3	1½
1.4	1⅝
1.5	1¾
1.7	1⅞
1.9	2
2	2¼

BLOCK CONVERSIONS

It makes sense to work with the nearest practical equivalent size, rather than an 'exact' conversion. For example, a 30 cm finished block converted exactly would yield a 11¹³⁄₁₆ inch block. However, the subdivision for the component pieces will be easier to work out if the finished block is translated into a 12 inch square. The difference to the final size is not significant and may be compensated for by rationalising the border sizes to the nearest sensible higher value.

Draw out a block on metric graph paper, using the conversions listed. Measure each component in the block and add seam allowances to it on all sides, to determine the requisite size unit.

SUGGESTED BLOCK CONVERSIONS

7.5 cm = 3 in (three units each 2.5 cm)
12.5 cm = 5 in (the conversion yields a slightly smaller unit than the metric equivalent)
15 cm = 6 in
18 cm = 7 in (the conversion yields a slightly smaller unit than the metric equivalent)
20 cm = 8 in
23 cm = 9 in (the conversion yields a slightly smaller unit than the metric equivalent)
25 cm = 10 in
28 cm = 11 in
30 cm = 12 in

1 To determine the required imperial measurements for border widths or sashing strips, measure the width then subtract 1.5 cm for two seam allowances. For example, an 11.5cm-wide border minus 0.75 cm seam allowances will convert to a finished metric measurement of 10 cm.

2 Convert the metric measurement to imperial. The conversion will be 4 inches.

3 Add imperial seam allowances to each side following the suggestions in the Seam Allowances box to the left.

SEAM ALLOWANCES

♦ All projects in this book include 0.75 cm seam allowances unless otherwise stated. This is slightly larger than the ¼ inch imperial seam allowance commonly used for patchwork.

♦ Choose an imperial plastic cutting ruler marked with inches, ¼ inches and preferably ⅛-inch divisions.

♦ For quick-piecing half-square triangles, add to the finished block size ⅞ inch for all required imperial seam allowances.

♦ For quick-piecing quarter-square triangles add on 1¼ inches to your finished block size for all necessary seam allowances.

Making and Using Templates

....

Always begin with a full-size draft of the design or block to be sewn. Label each shape with a letter or number and mark with the grain line of the pieces. Have the straight grain of the fabric parallel to the edges of the block. Keep this master draft of the block or design to use as a reference at any stage of the work.

MATERIALS FOR MAKING TEMPLATES

♦ Template plastic or cardboard (plastic is more durable and should be chosen if a shape will be used many times over)
♦ Ruler
♦ Fine-line permanent marker
♦ Craft knife or scissors
♦ Pencil
♦ Glue stick

HELPFUL HINTS

♦ Mark the wrong side of plastic templates with a dab of coloured nail polish.

♦ To prevent templates from shifting on fabric, glue sandpaper to the back.

♦ To prolong the life of cardboard templates, seal the edges with a coat of clear nail polish.

TEMPLATES FOR HAND PIECING

> Templates for hand piecing do not include a seam allowance.

1 **To make a template with template plastic,** place the see-through plastic over a full-size draft of the block. Using a fine-line marker, trace one of each shape required. Cut the shapes exactly on the marker line without adding seams.

2 Check that the templates you have made fit the master draft. If they are inaccurate, the mistake will be compounded as you sew the quilt.

3 Label the template and add the grain line on the wrong side of the template. For cutting, the template will be placed wrong side up on the wrong side of the fabric.

4 **To make cardboard templates,** first make a copy of the draft block, then carefully cut apart the paper copy.

5 Turn over each piece before gluing to cardboard. Cut out the cardboard shapes without adding any seam allowances.

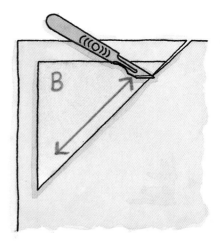

6 Check that the templates fit your master draft. Label the pieces and transfer the grain line of each to the appropriate template. Many quilters also add the number of times the shape must be cut.

TEMPLATES FOR MACHINE PIECING

> Templates for machine piecing include 0.75 cm seam allowances.

1 **Using template plastic**, proceed as for making hand-piecing templates; however, add a 0.75 cm seam allowance on all sides of your tracing outline. Cut out the shapes carefully along the new outline. Check against the master draft and label.

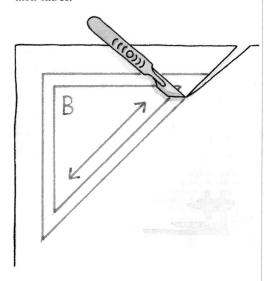

2 **To make cardboard templates**, also proceed as above but glue the shapes 1.5 cm apart to allow for a 0.75 cm seam allowance on all sides of each shape. Cut out along the new outline. Check against the master draft and label.

TEMPLATES FOR HAND APPLIQUÉ

To make plastic or cardboard templates for hand appliqué, follow the directions for hand piecing. Do not turn them over before labelling. In appliqué, the templates are placed on the right side of the fabric ready for marking.

If you are working with light-coloured fabrics, trace the shape directly onto the right side of the fabric from the master pattern.

WINDOW TEMPLATES

A window template provides you with a seam line and a cutting line in one template. It is also a useful device for viewing fabric motifs.

Make a template as for machine piecing with accurate 0.75 cm seam allowances but do not turn the shape over. Cut out the shape from the centre of the template to leave a window with a 0.75 cm frame.

REGISTER, OR REPEAT, TEMPLATES

Make a plastic register, or repeat, template if you want to put the same part of the fabric pattern in the same position in each block. For example, if you choose to use a floral print for the hearts in a project, and you want the same flower in the middle every time, it would be helpful to use a repeat template. This is not an economical use of fabric, so you will need more fabric than given in the materials list.

1 Depending on your working method, whether hand or machine sewing, make a template for the required shape.

2 Place the template over the fabric print as you want it to appear in the finished block. With a permanent fine-line marker, draw the outline of the motif onto the plastic so that each time you are able to position it correctly before cutting out the fabric.

QUILTING TEMPLATES

Make quilting templates from durable material, preferably template plastic, as standard designs are likely to be used for several projects. Follow the instructions as for making templates for hand piecing and remember to cut out the interior spaces.

Cutting

....

There are important differences in the way fabric is cut for hand or machine piecing and hand appliqué. Please read the directions carefully and practise on some spare fabric.

PREPARING FOR CUTTING

1 If you have not already washed your fabrics, do so before starting a new project. If you suspect any of your fabrics are not colourfast, see page 15 for further instructions.

2 Straighten the grain of the fabric by first pulling the fabric diagonally across in both directions and then again in the direction in which the fabric appears short. Bring the selvages together and press very lightly down the length of the fabric.

3 Trim away the selvages. If you do not, they will feel like hard ridges under your work. Selvages are tightly woven to stabilise the fabric and after washing often shrink, causing the fabric to pucker.

4 Steam-press all fabrics carefully before cutting. After washing, some fabrics become limp. This makes them difficult to cut; a light spray of starch during pressing can improve their behaviour.

5 Work out your cutting order and cut all the pieces for a project at one time. As a rule, cut the larger pieces first and work down to the smallest. Many quilters like to cut odd-shaped pieces from one end of the fabric, keeping the other end intact for cutting long strips.

CUTTING FOR HAND PIECING

1 Lay the prepared fabric right side down on a flat surface. Place your templates on the wrong side of the fabric, allowing space for the 0.75 cm seam allowances on all sides of the shapes. With a sharp pencil, trace around the shape. On dark fabric use a white or light-coloured pencil or a sharpened sliver of dry soap. Keep the pencil angled well in towards the template edges for accuracy.

If the fabric is unstable and slides on your work surface, place it on top of a sheet of fine sandpaper before marking.

2 Cut out the shapes, adding the 0.75 cm seam allowance by eye.

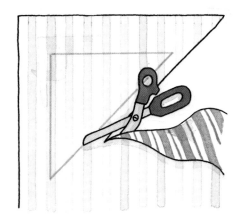

CUTTING FOR MACHINE PIECING

1 Place your templates on the wrong side of the fabric and with a well-sharpened pencil draw carefully around each template. Unlike templates for hand piecing, machine-piecing templates include seam allowances in the measurements, so you can place templates adjacent to each other.

2 Cut carefully – and exactly – on the pencil line; if you can still see the pencil line after cutting, the piece will be a fraction too large and this error will be compounded as the work progresses. If you have lost the pencil line, then your piece will be too small.

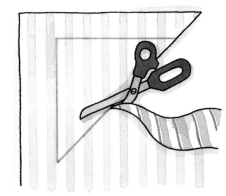

CUTTING FOR HAND APPLIQUÉ

1 Place the prepared fabric on a flat surface, right side up, and carefully draw around the template. Or, if using a light-coloured fabric, place over the design and trace off.

2 Leave enough space between shapes to add by eye a scant 0.75 cm on all sides as you cut.

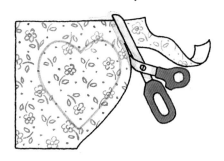

ROTARY CUTTING

The use of rotary cutters in conjunction with plastic rotary rulers and self-healing cutting mats has revolutionised quilt making. It is a fast and accurate method that allows you to cut through up to eight layers of fabric with a single pass of the blade. Even a beginner working on a single layer of fabric and cutting one piece at a time will find the process easy.

Rotary cutting entails cutting strips and cutting the strips into smaller units, such as squares, rectangles, triangles, and diamonds. As a result of this method of strip-cutting, a number of speed-piecing techniques have developed. *(See pages 44–63 in the Patchwork section for further information.)*

Rotary cutting saves you time, but you can just as quickly cut up lots of fabric incorrectly, so choose a piece of fabric you are willing to sacrifice for a practice session.

The instructions are given for right-handed quilters. If you are left-handed, you will have to reverse all the instructions.

Preparation for Cutting Strips

All fabrics should be prepared in the following way to ensure starting with a truly squared piece of fabric. Even with practice, it is not unusual when cutting large numbers of pieces to find strips beginning to drift, so be prepared to square up the end of the fabric again if necessary. This preparatory precision is essential for accurate results.

1 Press a piece of fabric that without folding almost fits the mat.

2 Find one side of the fabric that is true to the grain, such as the selvage, and align it with one of the grid lines printed on the mat.

3 Trim away the selvage by placing the ruler over the fabric with the right-hand edge of the ruler parallel to the selvage and 0.75 cm away from it. Hold the ruler down with your left hand without shifting its position. Place your ring finger against the left-hand edge of the ruler to help keep the ruler in place.

ESTABLISH GOOD WORK HABITS

♦ The cutter has an exceptionally sharp blade. Never lay it down without engaging the safety guard.

♦ Always roll the cutter away from yourself.

♦ Make sure the mat is clear of unwanted objects, such as pins, before spreading out the fabric for cutting. Rolling over a pin will permanently damage the blade.

♦ Practise presenting the cutter towards the side of the ruler from the

side, just above the surface of the mat, rather than with a chopping action from above. This prevents it from catching on the edge or corner of the plastic ruler, which damages both cutter and ruler.

♦ When cutting fabric, take care not to let the cutter run off the edge of the mat; this will damage the blade and the surface beneath.

♦ Never leave the mat against anything warm, such as a radiator, or in direct sunlight, as it will warp.

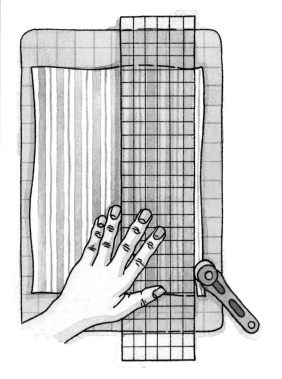

4 With the cutter in your right hand, flat side towards the ruler, disengage the guard. Start cutting at the edge of the fabric by positioning the cutter to the right of the ruler, almost touching the uncovered mat. Bring the side of the blade towards the side of the ruler; only when it touches the ruler should you put the blade down on the mat. This avoids damage to both the blade and the ruler. With the cutter at a 45° angle to the mat, roll it away from you across the fabric. Only a slight downward pressure is needed. It takes practice to maintain an even pressure.

Variation in pressure during cutting can result in uncut sections. Slight pressure towards the left keeps the blade against the ruler, but too much pressure can push the ruler out of place.

5 When you have cut the fabric, close the guard carefully and, without disturbing the fabric, slide the ruler away to the left and remove the trimmings.

6 To straighten a side adjacent to the trimmed selvage ready for cutting strips, turn the mat 90° and place the right-hand edge of the ruler close to the right-hand side of the fabric. Also align one of the cross lines on the ruler with the trimmed selvage edge. Cut across the fabric away from yourself. You should now have a good straight edge from which to cut additional strips.

7 To avoid disturbing your now carefully prepared fabric, simply turn the cutting mat around so that the trimmed end is on the left-hand side. Position your ruler on the edge of the fabric at the desired width to cut your strips. Proceed to cut as in step 4 *(see drawing at top of next column)*.

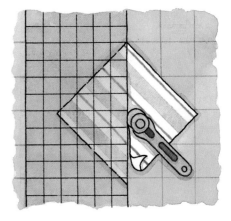

Cutting a Single Layer of Fabric

Cutting squares Carefully position one of your strips against a grid line on the mat to make sure it is straight. Place the ruler over the left-hand end of the strip at the required width. Check that the line is at right angles to the long sides of the strip before cutting off the first square.

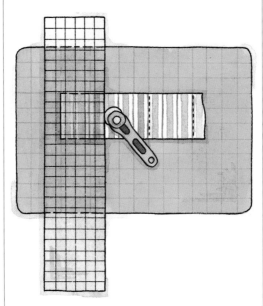

Cutting half-square triangles First cut a square *(see above)*, then position it so that two opposite corners align with a grid line on the mat. Place your ruler along the same line and carefully

cut the square diagonally into two right-angle triangles.

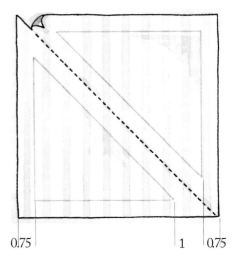

To estimate the size of square needed to cut a half-square triangle with the necessary 0.75 cm seam allowances on all three sides, add 2.5 cm to each of the two short sides of the triangle.

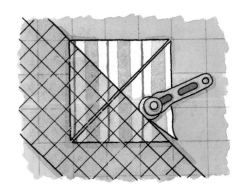

| 0.75 | 1 | 0.75 |

Cutting quarter-square triangles These are made by cutting a square across both diagonals.

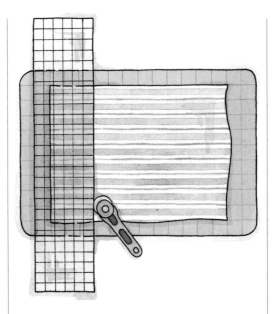

To estimate the size of square needed to cut a quarter-square triangle, add 3.5 cm to the long side of the full-size triangle.

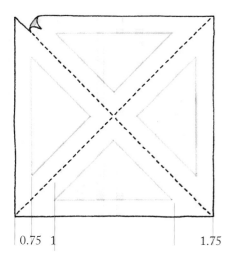

0.75 1   1.75

Cutting Diamonds To estimate the width of strip needed for cutting diamonds, draw a 0.75 cm outline around your pattern and measure the distance between the parallel lines. This distance will be the width of strip you need to cut.

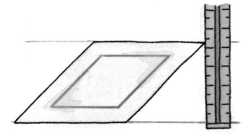

Make a paper template of the diamond and attach it to the underside of your plastic ruler. Use it as a marker for cutting.

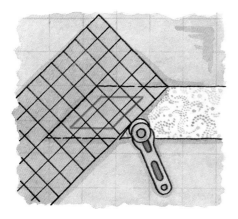

CUTTING IRREGULAR SHAPES

For more unusual shapes, a template will also be needed. Place the template on the strip and mark and cut in the traditional way.

Cutting Several Layers of Fabric

A small cutter with a sharp blade can cut up to six layers of fabric; a large cutter can cut up to eight.

1 Press the fabrics to remove any creases.

2 When cutting just two separate pieces of fabric, place one over the other and press so that they briefly 'stick' together.

If you are cutting a large piece of fabric, you will need to fold it several times to fit the mat. When there is only a single fold, place the fold to face you. If the fabric is too wide to be folded only once, fold it concertina-style until it fits your mat.

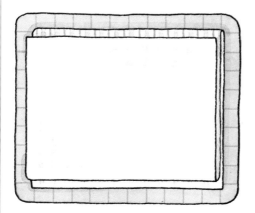

To ensure that your cut strips are straight and even, the folds must be placed exactly parallel to the straight edges of the fabric and you must cut at right angles to both the cut edges and the folds.

3 To cut, follow step 4 in *Preparation for Cutting Strips* on page 21. The more layers you cut, the greater the downward pressure you need to apply to the blade. The pressure must remain constant, or variations will result and the lower layers of fabric may not be fully cut.

4 Rotary-cut pieces are generally machine-sewn, but if you prefer to hand sew, mark your sewing line with a pencil dot at the corners of your pieces 0.75 cm from both edges.

5 Stack the cut squares neatly together. If there is a time lag between cutting and sewing, store them carefully in an envelope, plastic bag or small box.

STORING CUT PIECES

♦ Stack all the cut pieces together in like groups.

♦ Label the pieces, perhaps with a strip of paper wrapped around them, and place in a plastic storage bag; alternatively, thread all the pieces on a length of sewing cotton.

♦ Store the pieces flat, taking care not to fray or stretch the edges by overhandling the shapes.

Hand Piecing and Machine Piecing

....

The pieces for the blocks can be sewn together either by hand or by machine. Instructions are given for both methods, and it is acceptable to mix hand and machine work in a quilt top. The advantage of machine sewing over hand sewing is twofold: speed and strength. However, hand stitchers will vigorously argue that it is easier to match seams, sew curves, and inset by hand. Handwork is also portable; it can be picked up at any time, any place.

HAND PIECING

1 Pin the pieces together for a trial block, and from this decide on the sewing order.

2 Mark the pieces on the wrong side with a pencil outline of the finished shape.

3 Place the two pieces together with right sides facing. Insert a pin straight through (like a spear) from the corner of one piece to the matching corner of the other. Do this at both ends of the seam. Now insert some pins across the sewing line.

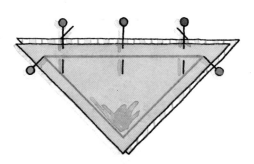

4 Thread a sharps needle with about 40–50 cm of matching sewing thread. Make a knot at one end and remove the 'spear' pin at one corner. Insert your needle on the pencil line 3 mm in from the corner and make a small backstitch.

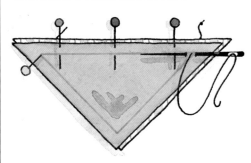

5 Sew small and even running stitches along the pencil line from one marked corner to the other. Try not to stretch the fabric as you go. Turn your sewing over from time to time to check that the stitches are on the pencil line on both sides.

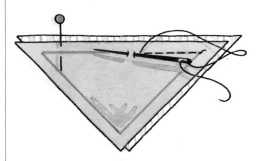

6 To secure the thread at the end, make two backstitches and then make several tiny stitches in the same place. This avoids a weak spot at the end.

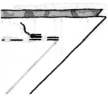

7 Press the sewn pieces as directed in the Pressing section on page 28.

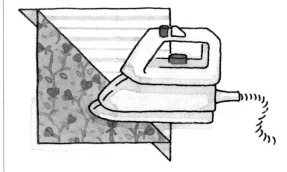

8 When sewing together pieced units, do not stitch across the seam allowance at the seam junctions. This will allow you to press the seams in any direction.

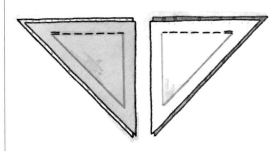

Precisely matching the marked corners, pass your needle through the seam allowance to the other side and proceed to sew.

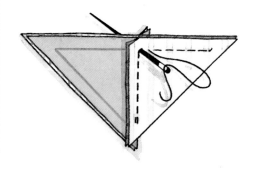

Detail of hand-pieced early nineteenth-century *Nine-patch* quilt worked in glazed chintz and floral prints.

MACHINE PIECING

The sewing lines are not marked for machine piecing; instead, the edges of the pieces are used as a guide for sewing. Therefore, to get the best results when piecing by machine, first check that you can achieve a 0.75 cm seam allowance consistent with your seam allowances established for cutting *(see box opposite)*.

Sewing

In machine piecing, the stitching extends into the seam allowances. This means that pressing as you sew is essential. You must decide how you want to press the seams at each step before you proceed to the next stage.

Below: Detail of nineteenth-century machine pieced *Dove at the Window* quilt

1 Pin two pieces right sides together with the pins at right angles to the line of sewing. Prepare several units at one time.

2 Place the pairs under the presser foot, right-hand edges against the guide, and, holding the thread tails to one side, start to sew. As the pieces pass through the machine, keep their edges level with the guide and let them feed through with as little steering as possible. Do not pull them through, as this will stretch the seam, especially on bias edges.

3 Chain sewing saves time and thread when you are sewing multiple units. At the end of the seam, stop sewing just beyond the edge of the fabric and leave the sewn pair in place while you feed in the next pair. The seams will not come apart

provided there are a couple of stitches between each unit. Press the seams of each unit. They can be pressed while joined, then cut apart.

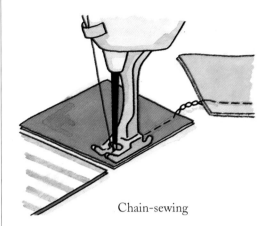

Chain-sewing

4 When sewing pieced units together, match the internal seam and ease as necessary. The block will look better if intersecting seams match, even if this means that the raw edges do not finish level.

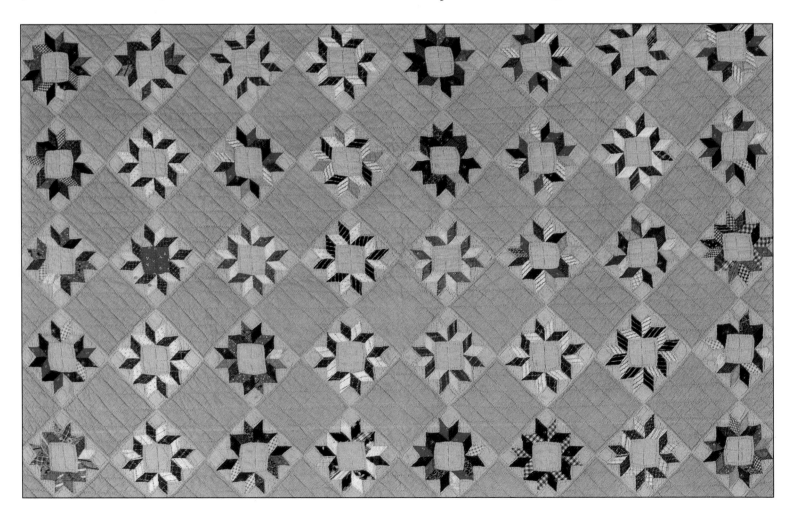

BASIC SKILLS   *Hand Piecing and Machine Piecing*

Checking the Seam Allowance

1 The sewing machine may be supplied with either a 0.75 cm foot or with a throat plate marked in gradations. In this case, simply check that these match your seam allowances used for cutting by sliding the ruler under the machine foot at right angles to you with the 0.75 cm mark directly below the machine needle. To make this easier, rotate the balance wheel by hand to bring the needle close to the ruler. When correctly aligned, lower the presser foot to hold the ruler in place and check by both looking and feeling whether the edge of the ruler and the presser foot are level or whether the edge of the ruler matches the mark on the throat plate. If so, these markings may be followed to guide your piecing.

2 Alternatively, position the ruler as in step 1 and place a strip of masking tape right against the edge of the ruler to use as a guideline. After

positioning the tape, you may need to cut a slit in the tape to allow the throat plate to be opened.

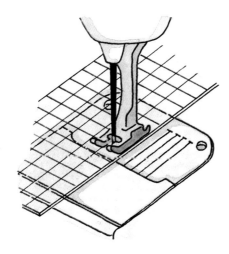

3 If you are cutting using templates, check the seam allowances in a similar way. On paper mark two lines 0.75 cm apart, ruled with the same measure used to add the seam allowances to the templates. Place the paper under the machine with the needle unthreaded and the right-hand line against the edge of the presser foot.

Sew along the paper a little, then look to see whether the stitching is along the left-hand line. If not, some machines allow the needle to be repositioned slightly to bring it to the required point to sew along the drawn line.

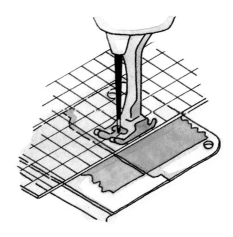

Alternatively, trim the paper to the right-hand line. Place test paper under the presser foot with the needle into the left-hand line. Lower the presser foot to keep the paper in place then add a strip of masking tape right against the paper as your sewing guide.

Easing Seams

Sometimes, blocks that must be sewn together do not come up to the same size. In this case, they must be eased between the matched seams.

To do this, have the longer of the two blocks facing you. With your thumbs, spread the fullness away from

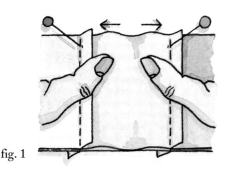

fig. 1

the centre towards the matched seams (*fig. 1*) and place a pin in the middle (*fig. 2*).

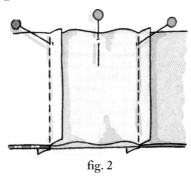

fig. 2

Repeat this to spread the fullness equally in first one half (*fig. 3*) and then the other half of the blocks (*fig. 4*). If necessary, repeat again in each of the four quarters.

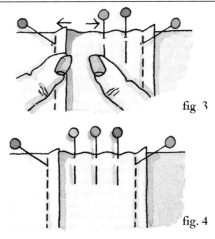

fig. 3

fig. 4

Often, the action of the sewing machine helps the easing process if the 'long' side is below and the 'short' side is on top. This is because the machine tends to stretch the top layer of fabric when two layers are sewn together.

Pressing

....

To do justice to your sewing, it is important to press your work carefully. Pressing for sewing is not the same as doing household ironing. To press, lift the iron and set it down on, rather than slide it across the fabric.

Whether you choose to use a steam or dry iron is chiefly a matter of personal preference. When using steam, take extra care not to distort the fabric. If you have a dry iron, a light mister will be useful for stubborn creases. To prevent fabrics from glazing, use a pressing cloth when pressing the right side of fabrics.

Press with the grain line; do not stretch bias edges.

PRESSING SEAMS

It is always good advice to sew a test block before beginning a major project. This will allow you to try different ways of pressing it to see which looks best. Sometimes, the same block will be pressed differently according to how it will be quilted.

♦ Press the seam allowance in the closed position first, then in the direction you want.

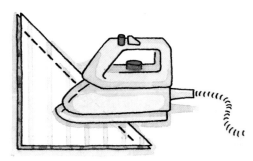

♦ Press the seam allowances to one side, not open as for dressmaking. This holds the seams more securely and prevents the wadding from 'seeping' through the seam.

♦ Wherever possible, press towards the darker fabrics. If this is not possible, reduce the dark shadow that will appear through the light fabric by trimming the dark seam allowance slightly narrower than the light.

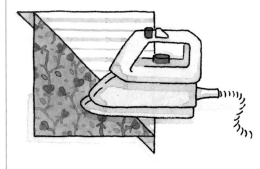

♦ If you have decided on your quilting plan, press the seam allowances away from the areas you wish to quilt. It is very difficult to quilt over the hard edges of seams.

♦ Always press seams before sewing across them in another direction.

♦ When joining fabric for additional length, press the seam open, as it will have less effect on the quilting design that may cross it. The same applies to strips joined for binding. Seams pressed open will cause less of a ridge.

♦ Sometimes a complex intersection of seams may not look accurate; rather

than unpicking the block and resewing, try pressing the seam allowances in a different direction. It is surprising how much improvement this can make. If you need to unpick a seam, first press the pieces closed again (right sides together). This makes it easier to get the seam unpicker into the threads with less chance of damaging the cloth.

♦ When a block has a multiple-seam join, press all the seam allowances in the same direction, rotating around the block, regardless of the colour of the individual pieces. This will help reduce the bulk.

Often, the piecing sequence for such a design involves assembling the block in two halves. Decide to press in a clockwise (or anti-clockwise) direction on both halves. When they are matched at the centre and stitched, either continue pressing the new seam to follow the rotation or press the final seam open.

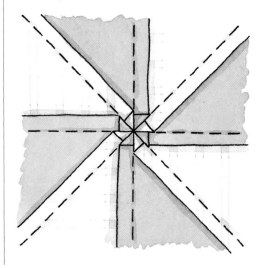

♦ Using a checkered fabric or a specially designed quilter's cover marked with a grid over your ironing board makes it easy to see whether a block is the correct size and shape.

♦ **Finger-pressing** is fast but not a permanent way of pressing small areas of fabric. Position the seam allowance, then press down on the seam. Move your fingers to a new position and press down again; continue until the entire seam has been treated. Take care not to stretch the seam by running your fingers and pulling along the seam.

PRESSING FOR APPLIQUÉ

♦ For a smooth finish, press your appliqué shapes before turning the raw edges under.

♦ To avoid flattening the sewn shapes, place a towel on the ironing board and cover this with a tea towel or pressing cloth. Place the work right side down and press gently.

PRESSING FOR QUILT ASSEMBLY

Deciding how to press seam allowances when assembling the blocks, sashings and borders is often a matter of common sense. The quilting plan may influence some decisions. For instance, if you plan to quilt in-the-ditch, the seams should be pressed in the same way for every repeat in order to achieve a consistent appearance.

♦ After sewing blocks together in rows, press all the seams of odd-numbered rows in one direction and in the opposite direction for even-numbered rows. As the rows of blocks are stitched, the alternate pressing directions will lock the rows together, making your work more accurate (*fig.1*).

♦ When pieced blocks are sewn to unpieced alternate squares, press the seams towards the unpieced blocks (*fig.2*). This also forms locking intersections when rows of blocks are joined.

♦ Appliqué quilts in which blocks are set side by side may have their seams pressed open. Quilted all around the appliqué motifs, the pressed-open seams will barely be noticeable.

♦ After assembling rows, press seams towards the top of the quilt.

♦ With multiple borders, press each before sewing.

♦ Press open seams in sashing or framing strips to make them less noticeable.

♦ Press seam allowances of framing or border strips away from the centre towards the edges of the block or quilt.

♦ Give the assembled quilt top a final thorough but gentle press before layering with the backing and wadding.

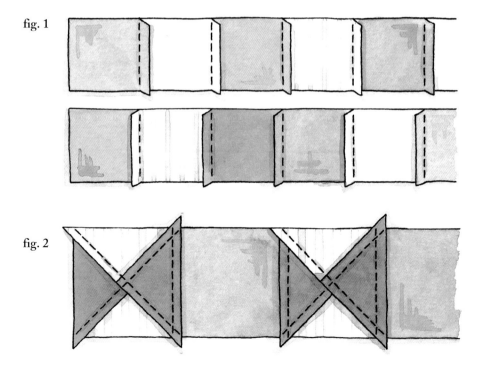

fig. 1

fig. 2

Assembling the Quilt

....

The quilt top is made by sewing the individual blocks into rows and then joining the rows together horizontally. The quilt pattern depends on sewing the correct blocks in the correct sequence, and also having them the right way up. Try to be methodical and always check your sequence before sewing.

JOINING BLOCKS

1 Press all the blocks and check their size. Each must measure 1.5 cm larger than their required finished size. This allows for the 0.75 cm seam allowance on all sides needed for assembly. Any blocks that are wrong should be either resewn or discarded. If your blocks vary in size significantly, check the following:

♦ different-weight fabrics used

♦ the grain line on individual pieces may not be consistent between blocks

♦ pieces were not cut precisely

♦ incorrect seam allowances used

♦ blocks were made over a long period and your accuracy has improved

♦ the seams have been pressed incorrectly

2 Arrange the blocks in their correct positions on a flat surface. Many designs, especially scrap quilts, allow

you a great deal of freedom in the placement of your blocks, so keep moving the blocks around until you are happy with the arrangement. If the quilt is intended for a bed be sure to correctly position the blocks to be the right way when it is on the bed.

3 Starting at the top-left-hand corner of the first row, turn block 2 over block 1 with right sides facing. The block edges should be level on all sides. Making a 0.75 cm seam, sew the right-hand edges of the two blocks together, starting at the top edge.

Continue sewing pairs together until all the blocks for row 1 are used. (In some designs, there will be an odd block at the end of the row.) If you are machine sewing, the pairs of blocks can be 'chain-stitched' (*see page 26*).

4 Sew the pairs of blocks together until you have completed the top row. Repeat the process to sew the remaining rows of the quilt. Press as directed on page 29.

JOINING ROWS

1 On a flat surface, lay out all the rows in order. Turn row 1 over row 2 with right sides together. Match the seams at each intersection with a pin inserted like a spear through the seams 0.75 cm from the edge.

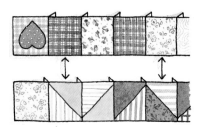

2 Insert pins at right angles across the sewing line and sew, removing the 'spears' before stitching.

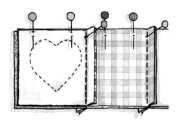

3 After sewing the two rows together, inspect the seam before pressing, as directed on page 28. Sew all the rows together in pairs, then the pairs together, until the whole top is completely assembled.

4 If your design includes **borders**, this is the time to sew them on. *(For detailed instructions on sewing and applying borders, see page 168.)*

5 If you choose a **quilting design** that requires the pattern to be transferred to the top, then it should be done at this stage of assembling the quilt. *(Refer to the Quilting section on page 156 for instructions.)*

LAYERING THE QUILT

Making the 'quilt sandwich' must be done on a flat surface large enough to accommodate the whole quilt. For large projects, you may find another pair of hands helpful.

1 A day or two before you layer the quilt, spread the wadding flat to encourage any creases to fall out.

2 Press the top thoroughly. Once it is layered, you will not be able to press the quilt again.

3 Measure the quilt top across the middle, vertically and horizontally. The backing fabric should be about 5 cm larger on all sides to accommodate take-up during quilting. If the backing is not big enough, either replace it with another piece or add an extra strip as necessary.

4 Press, then spread the backing right side down, smoothing out any wrinkles. Secure it to the work surface with masking tape.

5 Cut the wadding marginally smaller than the backing.

6 Centre the wadding over the backing and smooth out carefully without stretching it. If you do not

fig. 1

position it correctly at first, lift it up and re-position it; do not drag it into place across the backing. If you are working alone with a piece larger than you can easily handle, try folding it lightly in quarters, then start at the centre and unfold carefully.

7 Centre the quilt top right side up over the wadding. Again, do not drag it to adjust its position. There should be an equal amount of wadding and backing around all sides of the quilt top (*fig. 1*).

8 Secure the three layers by pinning and then thread-basting, or by pin-basting with safety pins. Start in the centre of the quilt and pin the layers together, working out vertically and horizontally, dividing the quilt into quarters. Fill each quarter in a

grid-like manner, placing the pins in rows no more than 15 cm apart. Release the backing as it becomes necessary. When the 'sandwich' is secure, thread-baste, starting at the centre and following the lines of pins. Begin each line of thread with a large knot. The pins can be removed a section at a time (*fig. 2*).

If basting with safety pins, remember that a large number are required for even a modest-size quilt. However, with safety pins there is no need for additional thread-basting.

9 To protect the edges of the wadding, fold over the extra backing to the front of the quilt and pin or baste lightly. This will protect the wadding during quilting (*fig. 3*). You are now ready to quilt!

fig. 2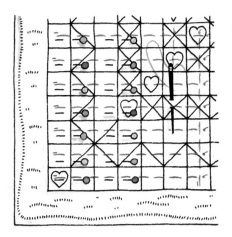

fig. 3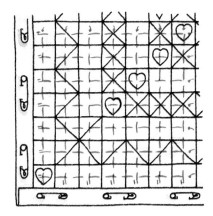

Hearts and Hourglasses

Skill level Beginner
Finished size 132 x 132 cm
Number of blocks 169

This attractive and simple quilt has been designed to introduce the beginner to all the basic skills and processes necessary for making a quilt.

The quilt is a mixture of plain squares, appliqué blocks, half-square triangle blocks and quarter-square triangle blocks (Hourglass blocks). The design elements can be modified or re-arranged. By changing the number of each type of block, you can give the quilt a different appearance.

Instructions are given for two simple speed-piecing methods for the half-square triangle blocks and the Hourglass blocks. This quick method of marking, sewing, then cutting saves time and gives accurate results. To make the half-square triangle blocks, always work with conveniently sized pieces of fabric, just a little larger than the area to be marked. Each square drawn will yield two pieced half-square triangle blocks.

The quilt can be made traditionally using templates, or the pieces can be cut using a rotary cutter and then hand or machine pieced.

There are several ways to prepare and sew hand appliqué. For this first project, I have chosen a particularly easy method of appliqué: cardboard pressing templates are used to prepare the hearts and a running stitch is used to sew them on. The cardboard for the pressing templates should not be so thick that it makes a ridge when the fabric is pressed over it, but be firm enough not to be damaged during the pressing process. The quilt has 17 heart blocks, so you will need two or three pressing templates. When one becomes distorted, replace it with a new one.

Materials

- 1.4 x 1.5 m-wide backing
- 1.4 x 1.5 m-wide wadding
- 40 cm calico or light-patterned fabric for appliqué backgrounds
- 2 m equivalent mixed scrap prints, solids and plaids for unpieced 10 cm squares, pieced Hourglass and half-square triangle blocks
- 25 cm equivalent of mini-dots in red, blue and turquoise for appliqué hearts
- 50 cm blue and yellow accent colours for half-square triangle blocks
- 40 cm red and blue accent colours for Hourglass blocks
- 25 cm red for binding
- Matching sewing and quilting thread
- Cardboard for templates
- Pencil and paper scissors for making templates
- Spray starch
- Cotton buds
- Pressing cloth

Cutting

- From the light-coloured fabric or calico, cut 17 squares, each 11.5 cm.

- Using the template provided on page 35, cut 17 hearts.

- For the binding, cut five strips 3 cm wide across the width of the fabric.

- From mixed scraps, cut 84 squares, each 11.5 cm, for the unpieced blocks.

Working the Appliqué Blocks

1 Using the cardboard, make a pressing template, without seam allowances, for the heart.

2 Protect the ironing board with a pressing cloth. Place the first heart right side down on the protected surface and centre the pressing template over it.

3 Spray some starch into a container – the lid of the can will do. Dip a cotton bud into the liquid starch and paint it onto the seam allowance around the template.

4 Using a dry iron set on 'cotton', press the seam allowance over the template with just the point of the iron. Press until the starch is dry and holds the turned seam allowance in place.

Work all around the shape, easing in the fullness on the curves as necessary. Fold the fabric into a neat point and press at the base of the heart. At the notch, clip into the angle just before pressing. Strengthen before clipping with a dab of liquid fray preventer.

Apply liquid according to the manufacturer's directions only to the area to be clipped. Prepare all 17 hearts.

5 Finger-press a light vertical crease on the background block. Use this crease to centre the heart, right side up, on the right side of the block, lining up the point and the notch on the crease. Pin or thread-baste.

6 Load a sharps needle with a 40–50 cm length of matching thread. Put a knot in one end.

7 Bring the needle up to the right side of the work from the back to 'hide' the knot a scant 0.25 cm from the prepared edge of the heart. Sew to the background using a running stitch.

Running Stitch

Try to make the stitches as neat and even in size and tension as possible. Pull the thread firmly to hold the heart close to the background fabric but not so much as to gather it.

At first, aim to get the stitches the same size even if not very small. When you feel your stitching is good enough, you can vary the appearance by choosing thread a different colour from that of the heart – perhaps a lighter or darker shade.

8 After sewing around the heart, turn the work over and work a few stitches neatly into the back of the existing stitches to secure the thread before trimming the ends.

9 Press all blocks as directed on page 28 in Pressing.

Working the Pieced Blocks

1 Press the two fabrics to be pieced together. Place the lighter one right side down on a flat surface and on it draw two squares, each 12.5 x 12.5 cm. Mark one diagonal in each square in opposite directions.

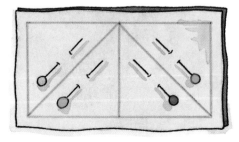

2 Place the marked fabric over the second square with right sides together. Sew along both sides of the diagonals 0.75 cm away. Sew continuously from one square to the other, and back again.

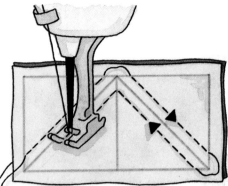

3 Cut along all drawn lines, including the diagonals between the lines of stitching. Press.

4 Work a total of 44 half-square triangle blocks in this way.

5 To make the Hourglass blocks, follow the directions for the half-square triangle blocks above, but mark the squares to measure 13.5 cm. Divide the units into two piles and mark a diagonal on one half of the units.

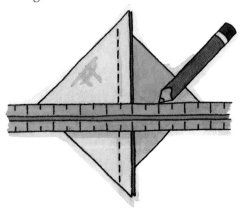

6 Place two units, one from each pile, right sides together, with the marked one on top. Check that the light and dark or colour contrast is the way you want it.

7 Sew along both sides of the marked diagonal, 0.75 cm away.

8 Cut apart between the stitching, open, and press.

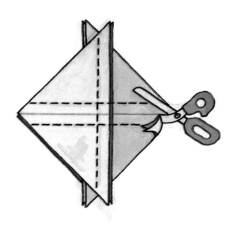

Assembling the Quilt Top

1 Arrange the 17 appliqué blocks, 84 unpieced blocks, 44 half-square-triangle blocks, and 24 Hourglass blocks using the plan on page 191.

2 Following the instructions on page 30 for Joining Blocks and Joining Rows, sew together the individual blocks into pairs, the pairs into rows, and the rows together to make the quilt top.

3 Assemble the quilt layers and baste in preparation for quilting *(see page 31 for layering and basting)*.

Quilting

Refer to the quilting plan on page 191 before quilting.

1 Hand quilt all around the hearts close to the edge of the motif.

2 Following the seam lines, hand quilt in-the-ditch of the Hourglass and the half-square-triangle blocks.

3 To quilt where there are no seam lines to guide you, place a strip of masking tape diagonally across each unpieced block and work your quilting stitches close to the tape edge.

Finishing

1 Seam together the five binding strips, each 3 cm wide, to make one continuous length. Follow the directions on page 171 for Single Binding with Automatic Mitres.

2 If you wish to hang your quilt, follow the directions below in Making a Hanging Sleeve.

3 Sign and date your quilt to finish *(see page 167)*.

MAKING A HANGING SLEEVE

♦ Measure the width of your quilt. Cut a piece of fabric to the width x 23 cm. Turn in 0.75 cm twice at both short ends and sew.

♦ Fold in half lengthwise, wrong sides together, and sew the long edge with a 1.5 cm seam. Centre the seam and press open.

♦ Centre the sleeve horizontally on the back of the quilt, at the top. Slipstitch to the back of the quilt along both long edges after the binding has been added.

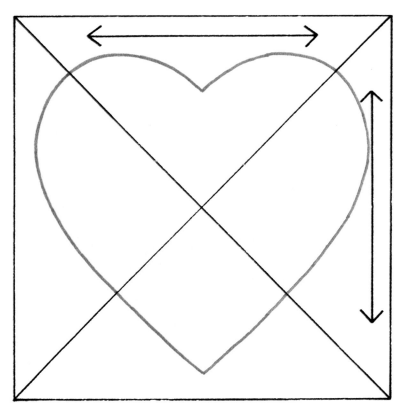

Above: Heart and half-square triangle templates

 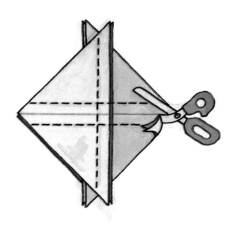

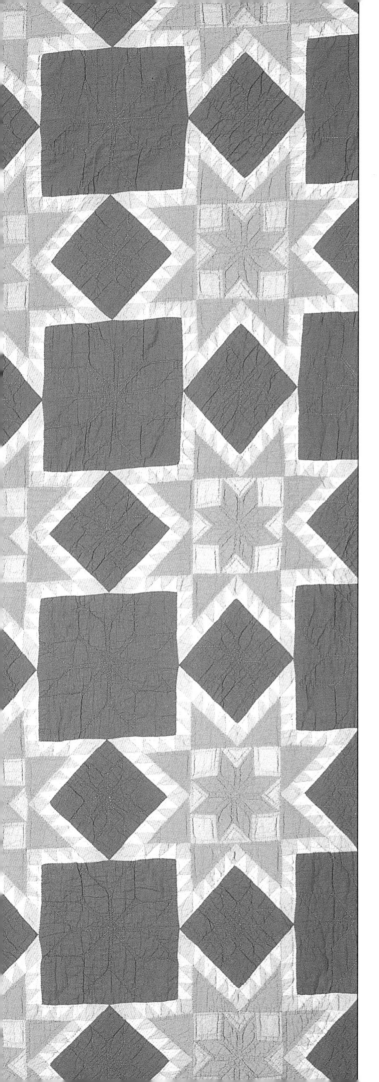

PATCHWORK

Patchwork, or piecing, involves sewing together, by hand or machine, pieces of fabric into patterns. Born of necessity, as a way of extending the life of precious fabrics in times when the process of cloth making was long and arduous, patchwork has developed over the centuries, especially in America, into a hugely popular craft, often displaying virtuoso design and sewing skills.

The perishable nature of textiles makes it difficult to ascertain how long patchwork has been practised. Joseph's Coat of Many Colours may have been a patchwork garment. We shall never know, but the universality of geometric pattern means that in more than one place and culture, people have translated small fabric shapes into a larger design for functional or decorative purposes.

In eighteenth-century England, the arrival of colourful Indian chintz helped develop an enthusiasm for bedcovers pieced with a single repeating unit. The hexagon, pieced over paper templates, was the preferred working shape, and this method is colloquially identified as English patchwork.

The art of patchwork, based on a sophisticated system of block construction, developed in America. Working in blocks is efficient in terms of both materials and labour. It does not demand long periods of free time or a large working space. The wonderful variety of designs and the inventiveness of the names given to quilt patterns demonstrate that no matter how simple their tools, early quilt-makers were as creative as any of today's stitchers.

The popularity of patchwork waxed and waned with fashion, often affected by social and industrial developments. It remained an active pastime until the post-World War I years. The belief that factory-made products were superior to homemade goods led to a decline in quilt making and the craft fell into neglect until the mid-1970s when interest in it began to revive. Today the enthusiasm for patchwork is global.

Left: Detail of nineteenth-century *Feathered Star* quilt

Library of Pieced Blocks

Choosing which block design to make can be as difficult as deciding on the fabrics; the selection is enormous. There are more than 1000 recorded pieced-block patterns to choose from, and, of course, you can always design your own. When selecting a pattern, bear in mind your skill level and the amount of spare time you have. The greater the number of pieces in the block, the longer the cutting and piecing will take, and beginners should avoid blocks with too many pieces. The size of your finished project should also be taken into consideration when deciding on a block design. For ease of sewing, the block size should relate to the grid of your block pattern. For example, four-patch designs work well on 10 cm, 20 cm and 30 cm blocks; nine-patch designs on 7.5 cm, 15 cm, 22.5 cm and 30 cm blocks.

Do not be surprised to learn that the same design is known by two or more names or that the same name applies to several different block patterns. Before the great revival of quilt making in the 1970s and the formal identification of block designs, blocks were named by the people who stitched them. Sometimes pattern names were incorrectly remembered or simply rechristened to reflect events and circumstances closer to the maker.

There are 60 pieced designs in this chapter to choose from as a possible starting point. The blocks in the library follow the custom of organising them according to the underlying grid over which the design has been drafted.

ONE-PATCH DESIGNS

One-patch designs are created by an aggregation of multiples of the same single units.

Grandmother's Flower Garden made with hexagons

Radiating Star made with diamonds

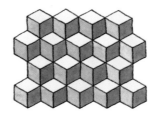

Tumbling Blocks made with diamonds

Land of Pharaohs made with triangles

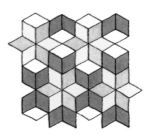

Stars made with diamonds

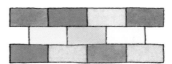

Brick Wall made with rectangles

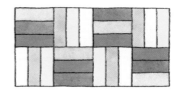

Rail Fence made with rectangles

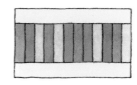

Chinese Coins made with rectangles

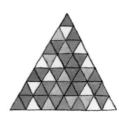

Thousand Pyramids made with triangles

Streak of Lightning made with triangles

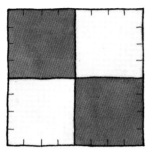

Four-patch

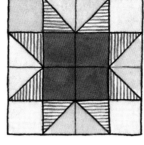

Variable Star

Postage Stamp Baskets

Pinwheel

July 4th

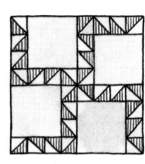

Century

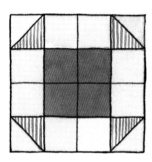

Puss in the Corner

Dutchman's Puzzle

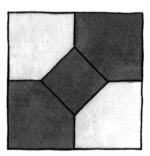

Bow Tie

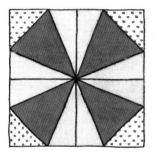

Kaleidoscope

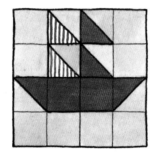

Sailboat

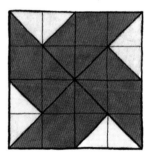

Whirlwind

Monkey Wrench

Devil's Claw

Broken Dishes

FIVE-PATCH DESIGNS

SEVEN-PATCH DESIGNS

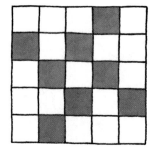

Five-patch

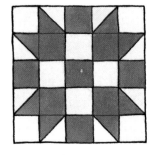

Sister's Choice

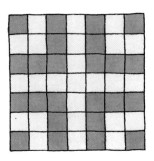

Hemstitch

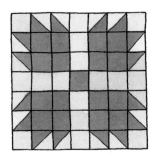

Peony

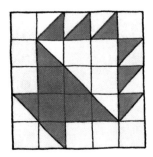

Broken Arrows

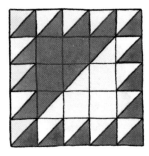

Jack in the Box

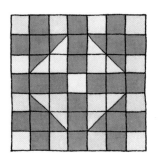

Stonemason's Puzzle

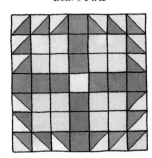

Bear's Paw

Cake Stand

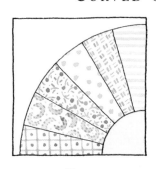

Lady of the Lake

Lincoln's Platform

Hens and Chickens

CURVED-SEAM DESIGNS

Moon Over the Mountain

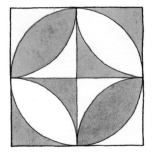

Fan

Dresden Plate

Dove at the Window

Mariner's Compass

Orange Peel

Drunkard's Path

Falling Timbers

PATCHWORK   *Library of Pieced Blocks*

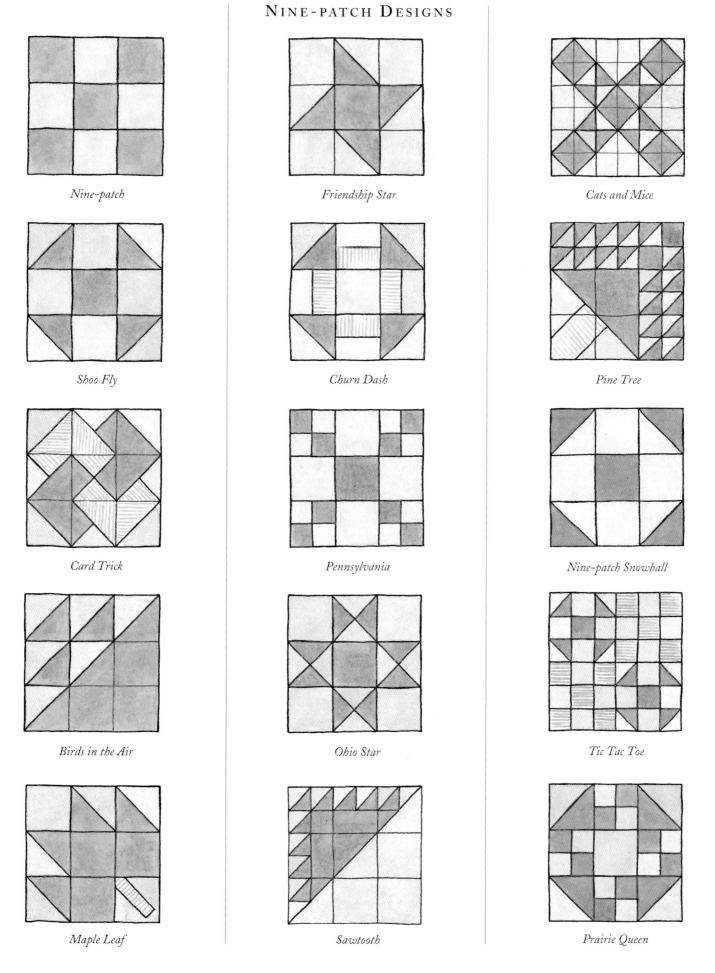

Nine-patch

Friendship Star

Cats and Mice

Shoo Fly

Churn Dash

Pine Tree

Card Trick

Pennsylvania

Nine-patch Snowball

Birds in the Air

Ohio Star

Tic Tac Toe

Maple Leaf

Sawtooth

Prairie Queen

Setting and Framing

Ask six quilters to sew the same pieced blocks into a quilt, and each, by choosing a different setting and framing, will come up with a different design for the top.

Setting refers to the way in which the various parts of the quilt top are arranged. There are innumerable ways in which the blocks can be put together, and each arrangement creates a different appearance. Blocks set side by side frequently create a striking secondary pattern. Pieced blocks alternated with plain blocks are an effective way of increasing the quilt size without a lot of extra work and offer a good opportunity for elaborate quilting that would otherwise be lost among the seams of a pieced block.

Framing describes the sewing of pieces of fabric around a block or group of blocks. Framing is a useful device, as it can unify blocks of different pattern, colour or size.

In this mid-nineteenth century *Underground Railroad* quilt, the secondary crisscross diamond pattern is created by alternating the colour and orientation of the blocks.

Using the simple two-coloured *Underground Railroad* block, the examples below give some indication of the variety of sets possible.

Single *Underground Railroad* block

fig. 1 Straight blocks set side by side with the same orientation.

fig. 2 Straight blocks set side by side with alternating orientation.

fig. 3 Straight blocks with alternating colouring and orientation and mitred framing.

fig. 4 Framed straight blocks with alternating colouring and orientation using setting squares.

fig. 5 Straight set blocks, alternating colour and orientation with vertical framing only.

fig. 6 Blocks set on-point, side by side with the same orientation.

fig. 7 Blocks set on-point with alternating coloured setting squares.

fig. 8 Blocks set on-point with alternating coloured setting squares and corner triangles.

Speed-piecing Strips into Squares

....

Quick piecing methods that make effective use of rotary-cutting equipment and the sewing machine are ideal for sewing numbers of identical units. The geometric nature of many patterns means that various combinations of strip-pieced squares and rectangles and pieced half-square triangles can be employed to reduce the time taken to work sets of blocks.

STRIP-PIECING TWO-COLOUR NINE-PATCH BLOCKS

1 Sew a pieced strip, using one colour in the middle and one other colour on both sides (Set 1). Press seams to the centre. Stitch the second strip from the opposite end.

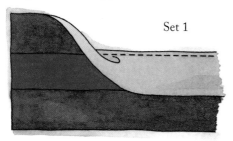

Set 1

2 Sew a second pieced strip (Set 2) twice the length of Set 1, reversing the colours. Press seams outwards.

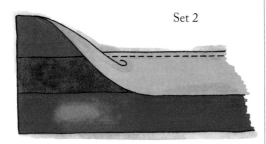

Set 2

3 Cross-cut the pieced strips into slices of the required width.

4 Matching seams carefully, machine sew the slices in the correct order to make the nine-patch block.

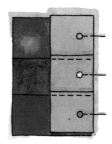

THREE-COLOUR NINE-PATCH BLOCKS

1 Sew together two pieced strips of your required width, following the illustrations below.

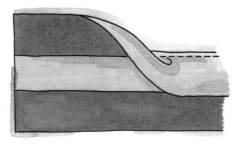

Set 1

2 Cross-cut and sew the slices together.

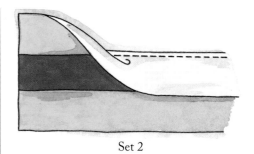

Set 2

2 Cross-cut the pieced strips and sew the slices together to make your nine-patch block.

FOUR-COLOUR NINE-PATCH BLOCKS

1 Sew together two pieced strips of your required width, following the illustrations below.

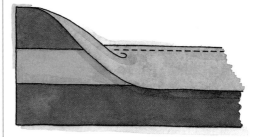

Set 1

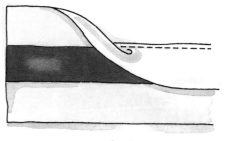

Set 2

2 Cross-cut and sew the slices together.

Double Nine-patch Quilt

Double Nine-patch Quilt

Skill level Beginner
Finished size 91.5 x 91.5 cm
Block size 22.5 x 22.5 cm
Number of blocks 5

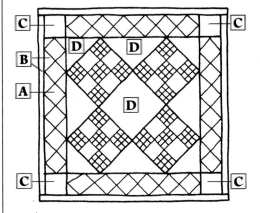

Materials

- 1.2 m backing
- 1.2 m wadding, 150 cm wide
- 25 cm red print A for border
- 80 cm solid red B for border fabric and binding
- 25 cm red print C for border corner squares
- 50 cm solid blue D for setting square and triangles
- 50 cm equivalent mixed yellow prints for double nine-patch blocks
- 50 cm equivalent blue prints for corner double nine-patch blocks
- Matching sewing and quilting threads

Cutting

Fabric A
- Cut 24 squares, each 9 cm.

Fabric B
- Cut two strips, each 4 x 96.5 cm, and two strips, each 4 x 91.5 cm, for the outer border.

- For the binding, cut strips 4 cm wide (1.25 cm finished width) for a total of 3.8 m when joined.

- Cut 10 squares, each 14.5 cm, and divide twice diagonally to make 40 side triangles for square-on-point border. These will have the straight grain of the fabric on the long side of the triangle to make a stable edge to the quilt.

- Cut eight squares, each 10 cm, and divide once diagonally to make 16 corner triangles for the square-on-point border. These will have the straight grain running around the right-angle corner of the triangle, also to give a stable edge to the border.

- Cut four strips, 4 cm wide and 18 cm long, for the centre nine-patch blocks.

Fabric C
- Cut four squares, each 12.5 cm.

Fabric D
- Cut one square, 35.5 cm, and divide twice diagonally to make four side setting triangles.

- Cut one square, 24 cm, for the centre setting square.

- Cut two squares, each 22 cm, and divide once diagonally for corner setting triangles.

Mixed yellow prints
- Cut four strips, each 4 cm wide x 66 cm long or equivalent length.

- Cut five strips, each 4 cm wide x 18 cm long, for the nine-patch blocks.

Blue print scraps
- Cut 16 squares, each 9 cm.

- Cut five strips, each 4 cm wide x 66 cm long or equivalent length.

Sewing

To make the blue and yellow nine-patch blocks

1 Using an accurate 0.75 cm seam allowance, sew the yellow and blue strips into two different sets with a different yellow print in each position.

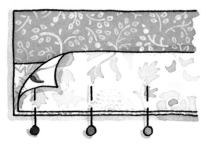

Set 1

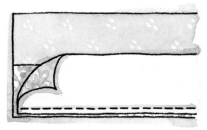

Set 2

2 Press the strips towards the darker fabric, aiming to get the seams of one set facing the middle of the block. The seams of the second set should face away from the middle.

3 Cross-cut into 16 slices, each 4 cm wide. If using a rotary cutter, match a printed grid line with the horizontal seam of the set to keep the cut end at right angles to the seams. If this end of the fabric 'drifts', true it up again before proceeding.

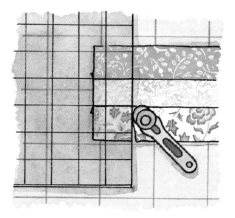

4 Sew one slice from Set 2 between two Set 1 slices, one from each fabric pairing.

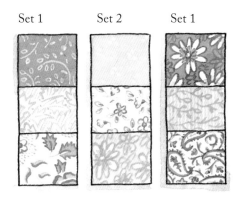

5 Press and check for size. Each block should measure 9 x 9 cm, including a 0.75 cm seam allowance.

To make the red and yellow nine-patch blocks

1 Sew the yellow and red 18 cm strips into two different sets with a different yellow print in each position.

2 Press the strips towards the darker fabric. The seams on one set face towards the middle of the block and away from the middle on the other set.

3 Cross-cut each pieced strip into four slices, each 4 cm wide.

4 Sew one slice from Set 2 between two Set 1 slices, one from each fabric pairing. Each should measure 9 x 9 cm, including a 0.75 cm seam.

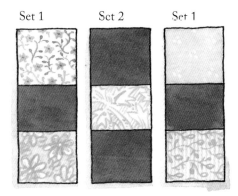

To make the double nine-patch blocks

1 Arrange the centre and corner pieced nine-patches with the unpieced blue print squares between. Sew these units together in rows.

2 Sew the three rows together to complete four double nine-patch blocks, 24 cm square including seams.

To make the pieced border

1 Attach one side triangle to two opposite sides of 16 border A squares as shown.

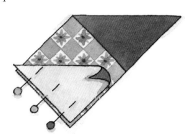

2 To the remaining eight A squares, add one side triangle and two corner triangles as shown.

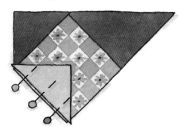

3 Arrange the prepared units into four borders, each having four step 1 units in the centre with a step 2 unit at both ends. Assemble the borders by sewing the remaining diagonal seams.

Assembling the Top

1 Arrange the double nine-patch blocks. Use the D fabric for the centre setting square, side triangles, and corner triangles. Sew in diagonal rows.

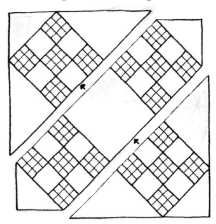

2 Sew one pieced border strip to opposite sides of the quilt. Attach a corner C square to both ends of the remaining two borders. Press, then attach to the top and bottom of the quilt.

3 Sew the two shorter outer border strips to the sides and trim as necessary. Add the two long outer border strips to the top and bottom.

Finishing

1 Mark wreath motif in the setting square, rosettes in the four corner squares and the melon-seed pattern in the border squares (*see page 188*).

2 Layer, then quilt, using a rectangular grid in the nine-patches. Quilt the wreath pattern. To finish, bind the quilt using separate continuous binding (*see page 172*).

Speed-piecing Half-square Triangles

A quick piecing method for half-square triangles is invaluable because this component is essential to many different block designs. It is integral to the Churn Dash, Ocean Waves, Birds in the Air, Hens and Chickens, Broken Dishes, Shoo Fly, Lady of the Lake, Variable Star and Sawtooth designs. The Crown of Thorns block simply requires only half-square-triangle units and plain squares. (For other examples, see the Library of Pieced Blocks on pages 38–41.)

This method ensures greater speed and improved accuracy. Working with triangles requires dealing with bias seams, which are not stable and are likely to stretch during cutting and sewing. Multiple distorted edges make precision piecing difficult.

TECHNIQUE FOR PIECING HALF-SQUARE TRIANGLES

1 On the wrong side of the lighter of the two fabrics, mark the required-size square, then rule one diagonal. Place your two fabric squares right sides together.

2 Using the pencil line as your guide, accurately sew 0.75 cm away on both sides of the diagonal.

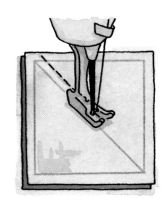

3 Following the marked pencil line, cut out the square, then cut the diagonal along the pencil line.

Cutting the square apart on the diagonal

4 Press the seam allowance towards the darker fabric and open to a square.

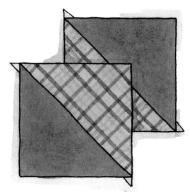

5 For making multiple half-square-triangle units, mark the lighter of your two fabrics with a grid of squares. Mark the diagonals in neighbouring squares in opposite directions. Follow the diagram for sewing directions.

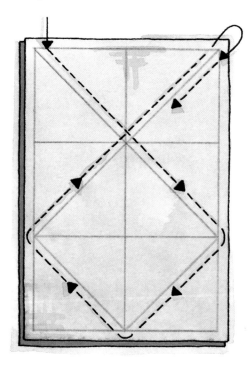

Late-nineteenth century *Ocean Waves* quilt. This complicated design can be successfully pieced
using the technique for half-square triangles opposite.

Skill level Beginner
Finished size 188 x 188 cm
Block size 25 x 25 cm
Number of pieced blocks 16

Materials

- ◆ 2.1 m backing
- ◆ 1 double-bed-size wadding
- ◆ 4.6 m black
- ◆ 2.3 m lilac
- ◆ Matching sewing and quilting threads

Crown of Thorns block

Cutting

Black

◆ For the borders, cut strips 19.5 cm x fabric width. Join to make borders 193 cm long for the top and bottom. Cut strips 19.5 cm wide to make two borders 158 cm long for the sides.

◆ For the side setting triangles, cut three squares, each 43 cm, and divide diagonally both ways to make 12 triangles.

◆ For the corner setting triangles, cut two squares, each 27 cm, and divide each once diagonally.

◆ Cut nine setting squares, each 26.5 cm.

◆ Cut strips 6.5 cm wide, then cross-cut to make 80 squares. First use up scraps remaining from cutting the preceding pieces before cutting into the main piece.

◆ The remaining black pieces will be cut later.

Lilac

◆ Cut strips 5 cm wide across the width of the fabric to total 7.8 m for binding.

◆ For the inner border, cut strips 5.5 cm wide. Join to make four borders, each 158 cm long.

◆ Cut 64 squares, each 6.5 cm.

◆ The remaining lilac squares will be cut later.

Sewing

1 Sixteen half-square-triangle units are required per block. Therefore, each block requires a grid of eight squares, each 7.5 cm, to be marked on the wrong side of the lilac fabric. Mark 16 such grids, one per block. Place right sides together with similarly sized pieces of black and turn into half-square-triangle units as directed on page 48. Press carefully.

2 Arrange these units with the plain squares of black and lilac to make 16 *Crown of Thorns* blocks. Sew units into rows; sew rows into blocks.

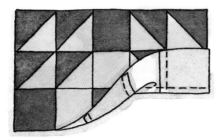

3 Arrange the blocks with the plain setting squares, the large side setting triangles and the corner triangles. Assemble into diagonal rows. Press seams away from pieced blocks and join the rows to complete.

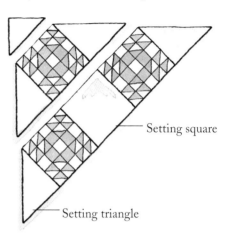

Setting square

Setting triangle

4 Attach the inner lilac borders with butted corners *(see page 168)*. Sew the short black borders to the sides and add the longer ones top and bottom.

Finishing

1 Mark the quilting design in the borders, setting blocks and triangles – a cable for the border, a wreath in the setting blocks and a floral motif in the setting triangles *(see pages 189–190)*.

2 Layer and baste the quilt *(see page 31)*. Quilt, starting at the centre, and work outwards. The *Crown of Thorns* blocks are quilted with a diagonal grid, which can be worked using masking tape *(see page 157)*.

3 Following the directions for mitres on page 171, use the 5 cm wide strips to bind the quilt. The finished binding is 1.25 cm wide on the front.

4 Sign and date your quilt to finish *(see page 167)*.

Speed-piecing Flying Geese

....

The Flying Geese unit is a pieced unit whose shape is a rectangle divided into one large triangle (the goose) and two small ones (the sky). It is a frequently used component of other block designs, such as Variable Star (fig. 1) and Virginia Reel (fig. 2).

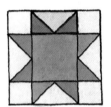 

fig. 1   fig. 2

The quick-piecing technique given here is based on a method devised by Pauline Adams and makes a set of four geese.

QUICK-PIECING METHOD FOR FLYING GEESE UNIT

1 From the goose fabric, cut one square. From the sky fabric, cut four smaller squares. To determine the size of the goose square, add 3.5 cm to the desired finished width of the flying-geese units. The sky squares are the height of the unit (always half of the width) plus 2.5 cm. For example, to make a 5 x 10 cm unit, the goose square must measure 13.5 x 13.5 cm and the sky square, 7.5 x 7.5 cm.

2 On the right side of the goose square, rule both diagonals. On the wrong side of the sky squares, rule one diagonal.

3 With the goose square right side up, position a small sky square, right side down, in the two opposite corners, lining them up with the drawn diagonals. Pin, then trim the tiny triangles from where the two squares overlap in the middle.

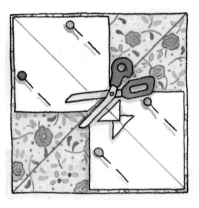

4 Attach the two small squares to the large square by sewing 0.75 cm away from the drawn diagonal on both sides of the line.

5 Cut along the diagonal between the stitching to yield two units.

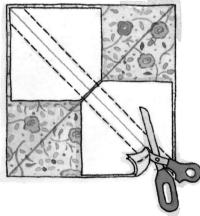

6 Press the sky squares away from the seam *(see drawing at the top of the next column).*

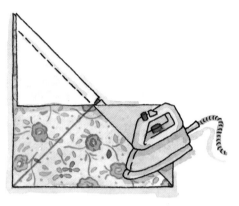

7 Place another sky square as shown in step 8, again matching the diagonal, and stitch along both sides of the diagonal 0.75 cm away as before. Repeat for the second unit.

8 Cut apart each unit between the stitching to give four geese units.

Four geese units sewn together in a vertical configuration with side borders.

Use the method opposite to piece star blocks like those in this early nineteenth-century *Variable Star* quilt.

Flying Geese Lap Quilt

Skill level Beginner
Finished size 104 x 122 cm

Materials

♦ 1.4 m backing
♦ 1.4 m wadding
♦ 1.2 m vertical border print used for top and bottom. If cut across the fabric, 40 cm is sufficient.
♦ 1.2 m setting fabric
♦ 50 cm calico for sky pieces
♦ 50 cm equivalent mixed prints for geese, none less than 14 cm square
♦ 25 cm contrast solid colour for 0.75 cm finished binding
♦ Matching sewing and quilting thread

Cutting

Border print
♦ Being careful to feature the printed design correctly on the strips, cut two strips for the top and bottom borders, each 14 x 109.5 cm. If necessary, modify the width to accommodate the print to the best advantage.

Setting fabric
♦ Cut five strips, each 14 x 102 cm, for the vertical setting strips and side borders.

Contrast solid
♦ Cut strips for the binding 3 cm wide, totalling 4.8 m in length when joined.

Sky fabric
♦ Cut 76 squares, each 7.5 cm.

Mixed geese fabrics
♦ Cut 19 squares, each 13.5 cm. Our example used one square of 19 different prints, but fabrics may be repeated.

Sewing

1 Following steps 1–7 on page 52, make 19 sets of four geese.

2 Divide the geese into four piles, one of each fabric in each pile if you use 19 different prints. Mix up the geese within the piles so that the same fabric will not always appear in the same place in a column.

3 To centre the points of the geese, lightly finger-crease at the centre of the long edge of a goose panel.

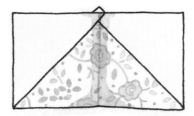

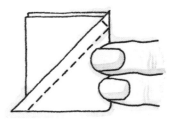

4 Sew the geese into four columns of 19. Use a consistent 0.75 cm seam allowance to make sure the apex of the goose triangle exactly meets the base of the next triangle. Centre this point

to the base of the next goose. Press the seams carefully.

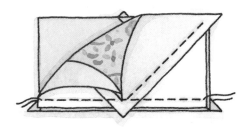

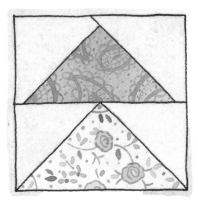

5 Sew the vertical strips of setting fabric and the columns of geese together alternately. Press before adding the top and bottom borders.

Finishing

1 Make a template of the goose triangle and mark the vertical setting strips with a succession of triangles, then quilt.

2 Quilt the geese in-the-ditch. For the top and bottom borders, quilt following the printed design.

3 Bind using single binding with automatic mitres *(see page 171)*.

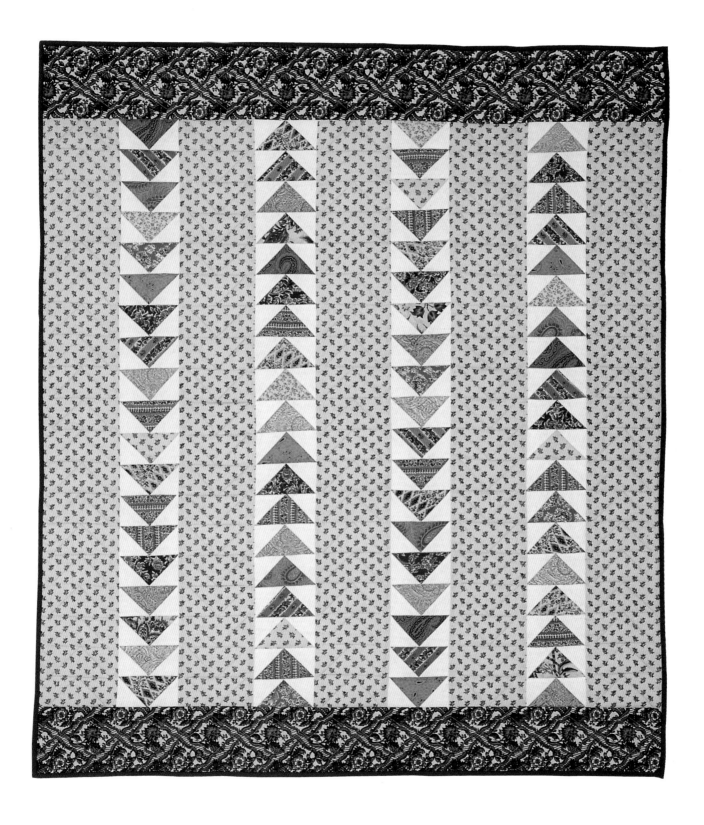

Speed-piecing Rectangles

. . . .

Although appearing less frequently than the half-square triangle, several pieced blocks feature a rectangle divided once diagonally to make two elongated triangles. When cutting with the straight sides of the rectangle on the grain of the fabric, the diagonal seam is on the bias, but not the true bias. The following instructions are based on a system, devised by Mary Hickey, that allows you to seam on the correct bias angle of the rectangle being used. It also keeps the grain parallel with the block sides. It is a fast method and, unlike some quick-piecing techniques, it is very economical in terms of the amount of fabric required.

SPEED-PIECING METHOD FOR RECTANGLES

1 On paper, draw a rectangle of the required size. Divide it diagonally once. Make a cardboard template of the triangle without seam allowances. This will be used to cut the fabric at the correct angle.

2 Make a second template in clear plastic of the whole rectangle, including 0.75 cm seam allowances. Mark the diagonal seam on this template, noting that the diagonal seam line will not coincide with the template corners when projected into the seam allowances.

3 Place two pieces of fabric right sides up, the lighter one on top. Work on a cutting mat. If the mat is too small, work step 4 on a table. Rule pencil lines, then cut with scissors.

4 Position the triangle template right way up, with its right-angle corner to the right-angle corner of the fabric. Place your ruler against the diagonal of the triangle so that the other side of the ruler reaches the top corner of the fabric. If the ruler does not reach the top of the fabric, slide the ruler and the template together across the fabric, keeping the lower edge of the template level with the lower fabric edge. Cut or rule a line at this point to establish your working edge. The cardboard triangle is no longer needed.

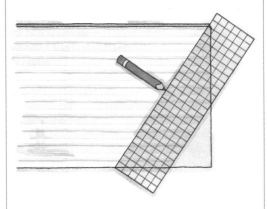

5 Cut off the fabric corner. Using the diagonal as the bias guide will enable you to cut strips at the correct angle to make rectangles on the grain. From the edge just established, cut strips the width of the short side of the rectangle plus 3 cm. For example, for a finished rectangle measuring 14 x 20.25 cm, cut strips 17 cm wide *(see drawing top of next column)*.

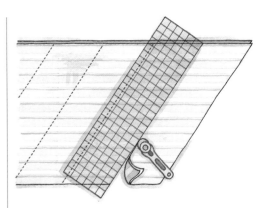

6 Sew the strips, right sides together, in pairs, one of each fabric, offsetting one against the other by 0.75 cm at the start of the seam. This ensures that the fabric is level when opened out. Press, then sew the pairs together again, continuing to alternate the fabrics, until all are joined into a single pieced fabric.

7 Place the pieced fabric right side up and position the rectangle template over it, aligning the diagonal ruled on the template with the first seam, as near to one corner as possible. Draw around the template. Slide the template along the seam until it just clears the first rectangle marked, then continue to mark and cut rectangles.

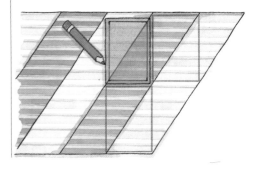

String of Flags Quilt

Skill level Intermediate
Finished size 183 x 223.5 cm
Block size 14 x 20.25 cm
Number of blocks 144

Materials

- 2.1 m calico for backing, 2.3 m wide
- 1 double-bed-size wadding
- 25 cm red or red/white stripe for 0.75 cm finished binding
- 14 m of 10 different mixed plaid and striped fabrics with no single piece less than 0.5 m
- Matching sewing and quilting thread

Cutting

Red or red/white stripe

- From red or red/white stripe cut eight strips, each 3 cm wide, across the full width of the fabric to total 8.15 m when joined together. Put aside for binding the quilt.

Mixed plaids

- Divide the fabrics into half-metre lengths. Group together in pairs, avoiding repeating the same combinations too many times.

- Draft a rectangle 20.25 x 14 cm and draw in one diagonal. From this, make one cardboard triangle template without seam allowances. Use it to cut diagonal strips as directed on page 56. Sew strips of alternating colours together into a pieced fabric.

- Using the rectangle template, cut 140 pieced rectangles.

- There will be triangles of fabric left over from cutting the diagonal strips, and from these scraps four more blocks can be made, using traditional hand or machine methods. Arrange the speed-pieced blocks, then decide which fabrics to use for these extra blocks.

Sewing

1 Sew the blocks together in horizontal rows. Matching the seams at the block intersections, sew the rows together to make the quilt top.

2 Press the top well and layer with the backing and the wadding.

Finishing

1 Quilt in-the-ditch following the continuous diagonals.

2 Trim the edges of the quilt before finishing with a 0.75 cm binding *(see page 171 for binding)*.

Speed-piecing Diamonds

....

Diamonds are a traditional favourite, but because of their bias edges, piecing is a test of skill and accuracy. Countless old unfinished star quilts are testament to the difficulty of piecing diamonds. Strip-piecing methods have greatly simplified the making of this design. The eight-point Star of Bethlehem is made up of seven rows with seven diamonds in each star point. Seven sets of seven strips are sewn, and from each set eight diagonal slices are cut, one for each star point.

STRIP-PIECING DIAMONDS

1 Arrange seven fabric strips in the required colour sequence to make up seven sets.

2 With right sides together and taking a 0.75 cm seam allowance, pin, then sew the strips into sets, staggering each strip by its width as shown in the illustration below. Press all sets carefully.

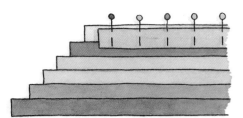

3 Place one set on the cutting mat. Position a quilter's rule with the 45° angle along one of the seams and trim the staggered edge before cutting slices to the required width *(see drawing top of the next column).*

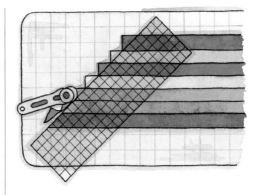

4 Cross-cut into slices of the required width.

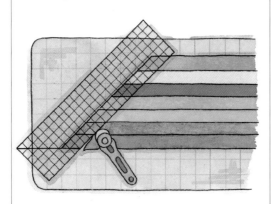

5 Sort the slices into the required colour sequence. With right sides facing and taking 0.75 cm seams, sew together, matching the internal seams as accurately as possible. Take care not to stretch the seams while pressing.

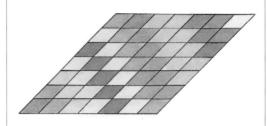

Right: *Lone Star* quilt

Star of Bethlehem Quilt

Skill level Advanced
Finished size 162.5 x 162.5 cm

Materials

♦ 1.9 m calico or sheeting for backing, 180 cm wide
♦ 1 double-bed-size wadding
♦ 1.9 m red
♦ 1.4 m violet
♦ 1 m navy
♦ 50 cm each turquoise, green, dark green and lilac
♦ 25 cm each dark violet and peach
♦ Scrap of light blue
♦ Matching sewing threads and medium blue quilting thread

Cutting

♦ Cut strips, each 64 x 5 cm, in the following colours and quantities:
 (A) light blue x 1
 (B) dark violet x 3
 (C) navy x 3   (D) turquoise x 7
 (E) green x 5   (F) dark green x 8
 (G) violet x 7   (H) lilac x 6
 (I) red x 5   (J) peach x 4

Navy
♦ Cut one square, 54 cm, and divide on both diagonals for the side triangles.

♦ Cut four corner squares, each 37 cm.

Violet
♦ Cut two strips 157 x 16.5 cm and two strips 123.5 x 16.5 cm.

Red
♦ Cut straight-grain strips 4 cm wide to total 6.5 m long for the binding.

Sewing

1 Arrange the strips in the colour sequences shown below and sew into seven sets, staggering each strip by its width *(see step 3 on page 58)*.

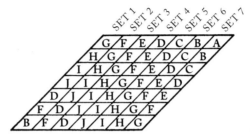

2 Cross-cut each set into eight slices 5 cm wide. Do not rush this step. Watch for any drifting and always true up the angle before proceeding.

3 Arrange the slices into their correct sequence and sew together to make the eight points of the star.

4 Arrange the star and sew the points together in pairs, matching the seams; stop sewing 0.75 cm from the outer end. Inset a corner square between the points *(see page 64)*.

5 Sew two pairs of points together; stop sewing 0.75 cm away from the raw edge. Inset a triangle between them as shown below.

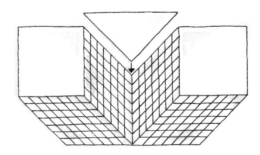

6 With right sides together and matching centre seams, sew the two halves together *(for advice on eight-seam joins see page 70)*. Stop sewing 0.75 cm from the end to allow for insetting the remaining two side triangles.

7 Sew the two shorter violet border strips to opposite sides of the quilt. Add the longer strips to the quilt top and bottom.

8 The sawtooth border needs 120 pieced half-square-triangle units in red and violet. Follow the directions on page 48 for speed-piecing these units. Begin by marking out grids to a total of 60 squares, each 7.5 x 7.5 cm, on the wrong side of the red. Assemble the pieced squares into two strips of 29 squares and two strips of 31 squares. Attach the shorter strips of the sawtooth border with the violet teeth towards the centre of the quilt. Add the longer strips to match.

Finishing

1 Mark the quilting design with wreaths in the navy setting squares and triangles, and with the cable in the violet inner border *(see pages 189–190)*.

2 Layer the quilt *(see page 31)*. Quilt in-the-ditch beginning with concentric diamonds in the points of the star. Work outwards to the wreaths and cable border.

3 Trim the edges of the quilt and finish with red binding using your preferred method *(for binding see page 171)*.

Seminole Patchwork

....

Attributed to the Seminole Indians of Florida, Seminole patchwork is a variation of strip-piecing. It is generally worked with narrow strips of solid-colour fabrics sewn into sets, then cross-cut and re-assembled into a variety of patterns. The patterns are frequently extremely intricate and require accuracy in matching and sewing seams. The traditional colourful geometric bands of pattern lend themselves to strong horizontal arrangements, generally spaced with unpieced strips of varied widths. The close proximity of seam allowances means that Seminole projects are usually lined but not quilted.

The best way to discover the diversity of patterns possible with this technique is to experiment. At first, practise with 4 cm strips with 0.75 cm seam allowances. After trying these patterns, experiment with your own ideas. Different patterns use different amounts of fabric. Since this technique does not use fabric economically, if you want to make something of a specific size, a sample is essential to ensure that you have enough fabric for your project.

SEMINOLE PATTERNS

1 Load your machine with a neutral-colour sewing thread and set a short stitch length, about 1.75 mm, to prevent the slices from coming unstitched when cross-cut.

2 Follow the basic instructions to work sets of strips as given for the

Double Nine-patch Quilt (see page 44) and try some of the more common patterns given below.

Two-colour chequerboard
Press the seam allowances on the assembled pair of contrasting strips towards the darker fabric. Cross-cut into slices. Turn alternate slices to bring the lower colour to the top. Sew the slices together in pairs, right sides together and using the interlocking seams (see page 29) to make a good match in the centre.

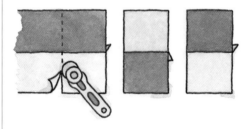

Three-colour chequerboard
Cut three strips from each of two contrasting fabrics. Assemble a strip of one fabric between two of the others. Repeat with the remaining strips to make a reverse set. On one set, press turnings to the centre and on the other, away from the centre. Cross-cut both sets. Assemble one slice from each set together, then join as above, keeping the pattern correct, to make the chequerboard.

Square on-point
Assemble a set of three strips, using either two or three colours but with the most eye-catching colour in the middle. Cross-cut into slices. When

joining, offset the top slice so that the first seam aligns with the second seam on the slice below.

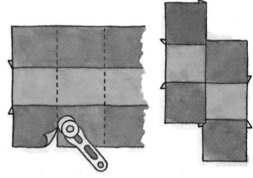

Repeat this offset when sewing the pairs of slices together. The pieced band will have a stepped edge. Do not trim until the neighbouring unpieced strip is sewn onto each side.

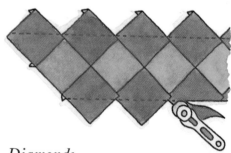

Diamonds
Assemble a set of three strips with a contrast centre and slightly wider outer strips. Use a quilter's rule to make the first cut at a 45° angle to the outer edges. Then cut slices of a consistent width parallel to this edge.

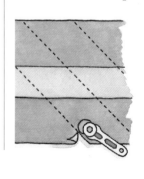
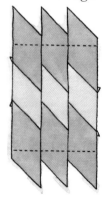

Seminole wall hanging

Sew the strips together to form diamonds of contrasting colour. The jagged edge will be trimmed when the band is joined to the next strips.

Chevrons

Assemble two identical sets of three strips. The outer strips should be slightly wider than the central strip. On the first set, use a quilter's rule to make the first cut, sloping to the left at a 45° angle to the edges. Continue to cut slices from this sloping edge. On the second set of strips, make the 45° angle cut slope to the right, then cut slices the same size as the first set.

Pair one slice from each set.

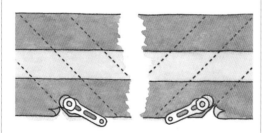

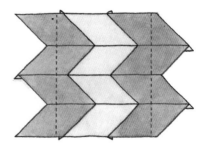

Insetting

. . . .

Insetting is required when you have to sew a piece into an angled space made by the joining of two other pieces. Popular block designs requiring insetting include Bow Ties, Cactus Baskets, and many of the star and diamond patterns. Each side of the inset is sewn separately, so hand sewing is frequently preferred. However, insetting can be done successfully by machine.

INSETTING BY HAND

1 Mark with dots exactly where the inset will be joined. Mark seam lines on the wrong side of the fabric.

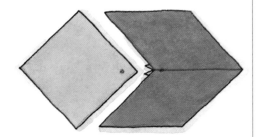

2 With right sides together and the inset piece on top, pin through the dots to match inset points. Match seams on one side from the inner corner to one end. Pin the seam.

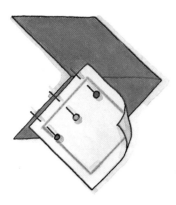

3 Starting at the outer corner, make a small backstitch to secure and sew the pieces together; use a short running stitch until you reach the inset points. Secure with a backstitch.

4 Remove the pins and fold the pieced unit below to one side, which allows you to match up the rest of the seam to the end. Pin, making sure that there is no tuck at the inner angle.

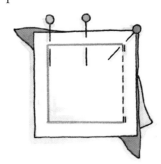

5 Without sewing into the seam allowance, complete the seam with a running stitch.

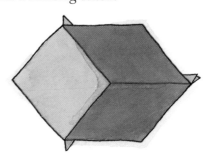

INSETTING BY MACHINE

With this method, the seam is sewn from the centre outwards in two separate halves to ensure that no tucks appear at the centre.

1 Mark dots and seam line as for step 1 of Insetting by Hand.

2 With pieces right sides together, pin through the dots. Pin the rest of the seam at right angles to the stitching line.

3 Set the machine to stitch length to 0. Place the patches under the machine with the seam allowances facing to the back, and manually turn the balance wheel to insert the machine needle into the inset point, removing the pin as you do so. Hold the thread ends to one side and sew two or three stitches – this will lock the seam. Stop, then reset to a normal straight stitch length and continue sewing the seam.

4 Remove the pieces from the machine and check the seam.

5 Fold the pieced unit to one side; this allows you to match the second half of the seam. Start with a pin at the inset point but now fold the seams the other way. Pin in place.

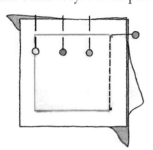

6 Set the machine to stitch length 0. Insert the needle manually into the inset point *(see step 3)* and sew.

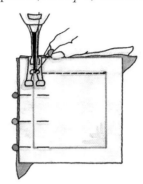

7 Remove the work from the machine, check the seams and press carefully.

PROJECT

Cactus Basket Wall Hanging

Cactus Basket Wall Hanging

Skill level Intermediate
Finished size 92.5 x 92.5 cm
Block size 23 x 23 cm
Number of pieced blocks 4

Materials

♦ 1.2 m backing
♦ 1.2 m wadding
♦ 1 m background fabric
♦ 25 cm equivalent scraps of four solid colours for baskets
♦ 25 cm equivalent floral and leafy scraps for diamonds
♦ 25 cm extra of one basket fabric for binding
♦ 1.2 m print for border (allow extra length as needed to match patterns)
♦ 25 cm accent solid or self-patterned fabric for narrow inner border
♦ Matching sewing thread and cream quilting thread

Cutting

♦ Make template G/Gr for the diamond and label points X for the outer edge of the block and Y for the centre of the basket.

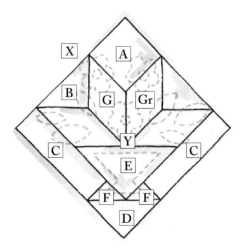

Background fabric

♦ Cut one 36 cm square and divide on both diagonals to give four side setting triangles. Cut one 24.5 cm square for the centre.

♦ Cut two 24.5 cm squares and divide once diagonally to make four corner setting triangles.

♦ Cut four 9 cm squares for piece A.

♦ Cut eight rectangles, each 5.25 x 17 cm, for piece C.

♦ Cut four 11 cm squares, then cut diagonally to make eight B triangles.

♦ Cut two 10 cm squares, then cut diagonally to make four D triangles.

Four different basket fabrics

♦ Cut one 14 cm square, then cut on the diagonal to produce large E triangles. Use one for each block.

♦ Cut one 6.25 cm square, then cut diagonally to make two F triangles.

Floral and leaf fabrics

♦ Mark the diamond template on the wrong side of each fabric. Mark four leaf and four flower diamonds with the template G and four leaves and four flowers with the template flipped (Gr). Cut out the shapes with a 0.75 cm seam allowance.

Accent border fabric

♦ Cut two strips 2.5 x 69 cm and two strips 2.5 x 71 cm.

Print border fabric

♦ Cut four strips for the borders. Measure the width of the repeat that you plan to feature. For instance, if the repeat is 15 cm, add this to the length of the centre panel, plus another 5 cm. If the centre measures 65 cm, then add 15 cm plus 5 cm to equal a length of 85 cm to be cut. The wider the border design, the longer the pieces to cut.

Sewing (to make one block)

1 With right sides together, sew two pairs of G-Gr, matching the points carefully and stitching along the marked pencil lines.

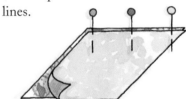

2 Inset a triangle B into each pair, matching the inside corners.

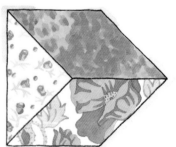

3 Sew these sets together and press the seams in one direction around the centre. Then insert piece A as for the triangle in step 2.

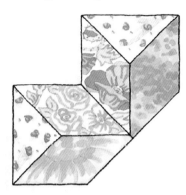

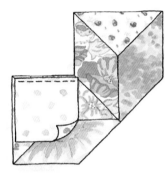

4 Lightly fold the basket triangle E in half to find the middle of the long edge. Match this point to the centre of the assembled diamonds and, taking care not to stretch the seam, sew on piece E.

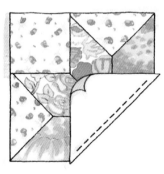

5 Attach one short side of a triangle F to one end of a C strip. Sew a pair of F–C units.

6 Attach one F–C unit to appropriate sides of the assembled basket *(see drawing at top of next column).*

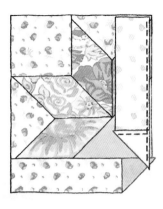

7 Lightly fold the background fabric triangle D in half to find the middle of the long edge. Match to the centre of the basket base, then attach piece D.

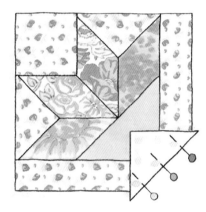

8 Make three more blocks, each with a different colour basket.

9 Lay out the blocks and put the side and corner setting triangles in place, making up three diagonal rows. Rows 1 and 3 are made up of one corner triangle and one basket block flanked by side triangles on opposite sides; row 2 consists of the central square with two basket blocks, each one with a corner triangle.

10 Matching the block intersections, join together in diagonal rows and press.

11 Sew the two shorter inner-border strips to the sides of the centre panel. Press seam away from the

centre, then sew the longer strips across the top and bottom. Press.

12 Match one short end of the first border strip with the top of the quilt on the right side and sew to within 15 cm of the end of the seam. Next, match the end of the second border strip to the top-left corner and sew in place across the top of the centre, continuing across the top end of the first border strip. In the same way, add the third and fourth strips, then complete the first seam by sewing across the end of the fourth strip.

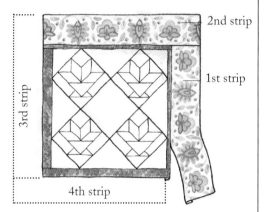

13 Mark the quilt top with a freehand arrangement of leaves and flowers over the diamond shapes.

14 Assemble the quilt layers as directed on page 31 and baste.

Finishing

1 Quilt the flowers and leaves over the diamonds. Quilt 0.75 cm inside the basket outline and quilt a diagonal 5 cm grid over the background centre panel. Quilt in-the-ditch of the two borders and follow the design of the main shapes in the floral border.

2 Trim the raw edges level with the quilt top and add a narrow accent binding *(see page 171).* Sign and date your quilt to finish.

Curved-seam Piecing

....

Curved seams have the reputation of being difficult to sew. Careful cutting out and preparation are just part of the solution; the rest lies in not stretching or distorting those curved edges. The best results come from doing it carefully and right the first time, as any resewing of seams leads to over-handling and problems of distortion.

Common curved-seam blocks include Moon Over the Mountain, New York Beauty and pieced fan designs.

MAKING A DRUNKARD'S PATH BLOCK

1 Using the *Drunkard's Path* block template on page 175, cut out A and B. Draw a sewing line 0.75 cm from the raw edge on the wrong side of both pieces to be joined. The curved edges should have a central balance mark, or notch *(see below)*. Matching these helps distribute the fabric evenly around the curve. These must be exactly opposite each other when the two curves are together. If working with long curves or when making large blocks, add extra marks equally spaced around the curves.

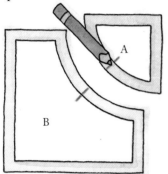

2 Place the two curved pieces right sides together and spear the central notches with a pin as shown below. The two curves appear as if they will never come together, as they face opposite directions.

3 With pins, locate both ends of the seam, exactly matching the 0.75 cm seam allowance.

4 Two curves will fit together perfectly at only one point – where the seam line is drawn. If the seam deviates even a little, one side will be longer, or shorter, than it should be, so stay exactly on the drawn lines. Work on one half of the curve at a time. Put a pin halfway between the centre and the corner on the seam line and push it through the piece below, also on the seam line. Repeat, putting pins halfway between the

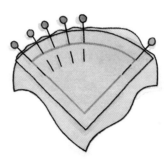

spaces until the gaps between pins are no greater than about 0.75 cm. Repeat to ease together the other half of the seam. Baste.

5 Sew the seam carefully. Some people like to hand sew curves, but machine sewing is faster and just as accurate. If machine sewing, turn the curve smoothly and stay on the line. Use a short stitch length which creates more 'give' and prolongs the life of the curved seam.

6 After sewing, inspect both sides. There should be no little bubbles or tucks. If the seam looks good, return to the wrong side and clip into the convex curve at regular intervals almost to the seam. Press.

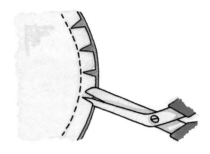

HELPFUL HINT

♦ Some quilters prefer to clip the convex curve before pinning and sewing. I advise against this because it is easy to accidentally sew through the end of a clip. It can also distort that side of the seam, making it very hard to match the curves.

Nineteenth-century *Drunkard's Path* quilt

Eight-seam Join

....

Some of the most challenging quilt blocks contain shapes that meet in multiple joins. An eight-seam join appears in such traditional block designs as Mariner's Compass, Kaleidoscope, Dutchman's Puzzle, LeMoyne Star and Century. With many converging seams, the join requires careful and accurate sewing.

The instructions given below are for sewing an eight-seam join on a Pinwheel block, but the technique applies to any block pattern with multiple joins.

Pinwheel with an eight-seam join

MAKING A BLOCK WITH AN EIGHT-SEAM JOIN

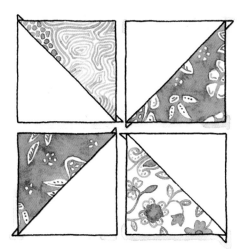

1 Arrange your basic components to make the block configuration *(see drawing in column 1)* – in this case, a pinwheel block. Make sure the pressed seam allowances in all four quarter-blocks rotate in one direction.

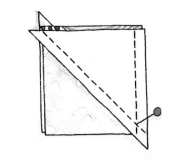

The wrong side of the top half of the *Pinwheel* block

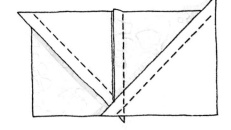

The wrong side of the bottom half of the *Pinwheel* block

2 Sew the half-square triangles together in pairs, matching the seam intersections.

3 After sewing two halves of the block, spear the centres with a pin, even if the ends of the seams are not exactly level. It is more important to have the centres match exactly than to have the edges of the blocks level. Pin at right angles across the whole seam and remove the spear pin before stitching.

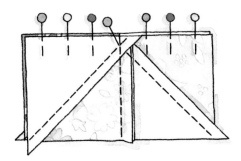

4 To check how good the match is, machine-baste about 2.5 cm of stitching through the centre join, using the longest stitch possible on the machine. Large basting stitches are easy to remove if the centres do not match precisely. If you are happy with the appearance of the seam, adjust the stitch length to normal (2–2.5 mm) and sew the seam slowly and carefully.

5 If you are sewing by hand, fold all the seam allowances in the same direction, swirling them in the middle to reduce bulk *(see page 28)*. If machine sewing, press the seams flat, with the final seam pressed open.

Opposite: Mid-nineteenth century *Union Army Encircled Star* quilt

Pinwheel Variation Quilt

Skill level Intermediate
Finished size 133.5 x 133.5 cm
Block size 30 x 30 cm and 10 x 10 cm
Number of blocks 4 large and 53 small

Materials

- 1.6 m backing, 150 cm wide
- 1.6 m wadding, 150 cm wide
- 1.3 m white
- 50 cm navy for binding and border
- 1.6 m total of mixed navy-and-white prints with a minimum of three different fabrics
- Matching sewing and quilting thread

Cutting

Navy
- Cut strips 11.5 cm wide and seam together to make two border strips 140 cm long and two strips 122 cm long.

- Cut five strips 2.5 cm wide across the full width of the fabric and join into a continuous length for the binding.

Mixed navy-and-white prints
- Cut four 17.5 cm squares and divide diagonally to make eight triangles.

- Cut four 7.5 cm squares and divide once diagonally to make eight triangles.

White
- Cut as for mixed navy-and-white prints.

- For the pinwheel blocks, the rest of the cutting will be done after sewing.

Sewing

1 To make the large pinwheel blocks, draw 12 squares, each 17.5 cm, in grids on the wrong side of the white fabric. Plan the grids to fit sensibly with the print fabrics being used. It will be more interesting if a different number of each print are worked. Mark one diagonal in each square, with diagonals going in opposite directions in adjacent squares.

2 Place the white fabric on the navy-and-white print with right sides together and begin making the half-square units.

3 Press the seam allowances towards the dark fabric. Set aside eight of the prepared half-square units for the side setting triangles.

4 Arrange the remaining 16 units into four groups of four. Have them turned the right way to form the large pinwheel and sew together into blocks.

5 Make up eight side setting triangles by sewing one large white and one large navy-and-white print triangle to two adjacent sides of the eight units set aside earlier.

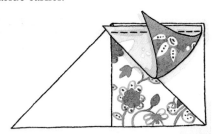

6 To make the small pinwheel blocks, begin by marking out a total of 108 squares, each 7.5 cm, in conveniently

sized grids on the wrong side of the white fabric. Work the pieced half-square triangles and press carefully before assembling sets of four to make 53 small pinwheel blocks.

7 To the remaining four small pieced units, add one small white and one small navy-and-white print triangle to two adjacent sides, maintaining the chequered effect. These units fit at the ends of the pieced setting strips, midway along the sides of the quilt.

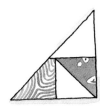

8 Sew the remaining small triangles in pairs of one white and one navy-and-white print to make the quarter units for the ends of the pieced setting strips at the corners of the quilt.

9 Arrange and sew the quilt blocks as shown below. Check that the side and corner triangles at the ends of the setting strips are correctly placed to form straight sides to the quilt.

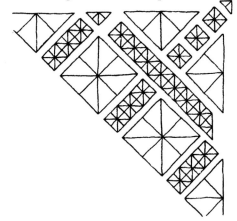

10 To attach the butted border, sew the shorter strips to two opposite sides of the quilt first, then add the long strips to the top and bottom *(see page 168)*.

Finishing

1 Mark the quilt top with broken curves for large pinwheels, cable for border and echo pattern for small pinwheels *(see pattern on page 189)*.

2 Assemble the quilt layers and baste *(see page 31)*. Quilt starting from the centre and work outwards.

3 Add a 0.75 cm binding. Sign and date your quilt to finish.

Log Cabin

....

The Log Cabin design is a simple pattern made by adding successive strips of fabric around a central unit. Although it is considered a particularly American motif there are primitive examples of the design as far back as the ancient Egyptians.

The design, which travelled with the early settlers to the New World, was probably renamed after the traditional pioneer homes. Economical in that it utilises the narrowest of fabric scraps, easy to make, and with limitless design opportunities, the Log Cabin block remains a firm favourite among quilt makers worldwide.

The most popular form of the pattern uses a red centre square – said to represent the glowing hearth – surrounded by half dark and half light strips, creating the effect of light and shadow. By changing the relationship of light and dark, you can create different designs.

MAKING A LOG CABIN BLOCK

1 From the template on page 174, enlarge the block to 17.5 cm. Trace the block onto a square of calico.

2 Cut a 4 cm red square and pin or baste right side up to the middle of the foundation.

3 Cut a variety of light and dark strips each 4 cm wide. Place a light strip right side down over the centre red square, with raw edges level. Stitch together, using a 0.75 cm seam allowance.

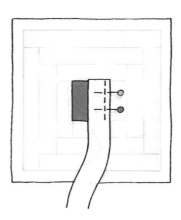

4 Trim away excess strip so that it is even with the centre square.

5 Fold the strip to the right side and press.

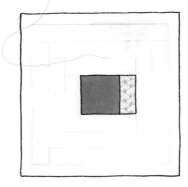

6 Add a second light-coloured strip right side down over the centre; sew, trim and press.

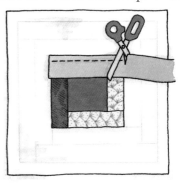

7 For the third and fourth strips, choose dark fabrics and attach in the manner outlined for steps 3–6.

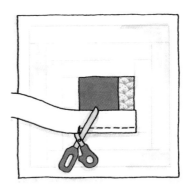

8 Continue in the same clockwise direction, adding the remaining strips to complete the block.

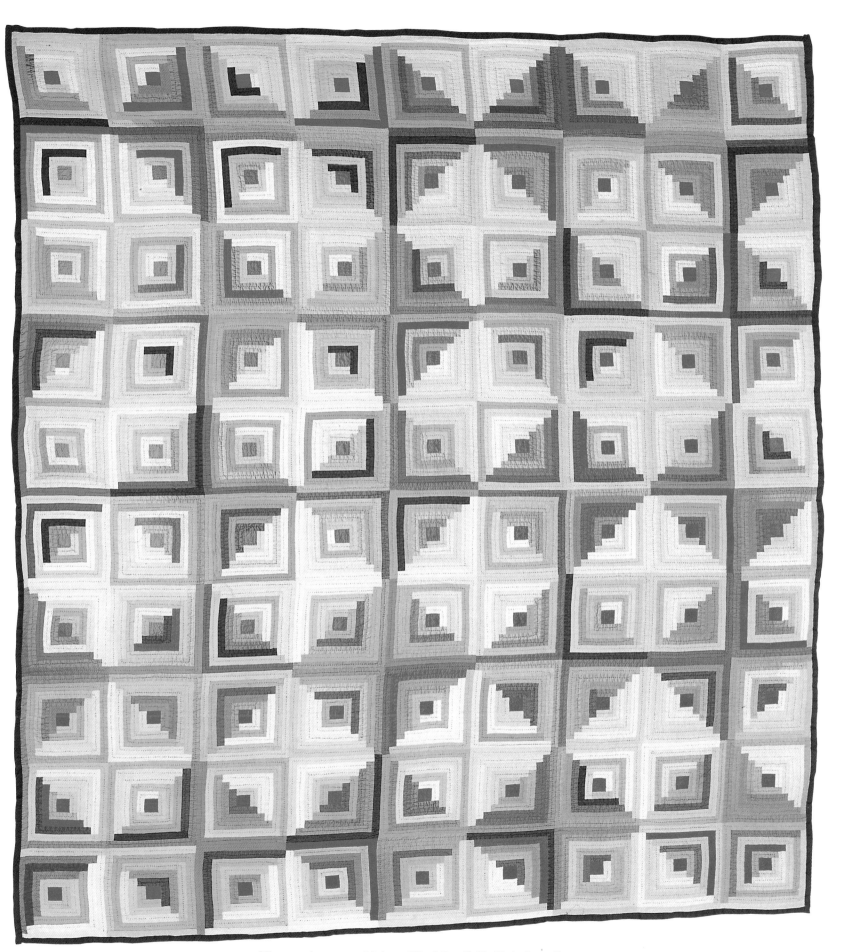

Nineteenth-century *Light and Dark Log Cabin Variation* quilt

Log Cabin Barn Raising

Skill level Beginner
Finished size 193 x 193 cm
Block size 17.5 x 17.5 cm
Number of blocks 100

Materials

- 2.1 m backing, 2m wide
- 1 double-bed-size wadding
- 2.3 m red
- 1.6 m each pink and white
- 2.1 m black

Cutting

Red
- Cut strips 4cm wide, joining as necessary to make four outer borders, each 196 cm long.

- Cut strips 4cm wide for the logs. From these strips, cut 50 squares, each 4cm, for the centres.

Pink
- Cut strips 4cm wide, to make four middle borders, each 190.5 cm long.

- Cut strips 4cm wide for logs.

White
- Cut strips 4cm wide, to make four inner borders, each 185.5 cm long.

- Cut strips 4cm wide for logs.

Black
- Cut strips 4cm wide for logs. From the strips, cut 50 squares, each 4cm, for the centres.

- Cut strips 5.5cm wide totalling 7.8m for a finished 2 cm binding.

Sewing

1 Following the instructions on page 74 for making a Log Cabin block, work 50 blocks for each sequence.

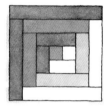 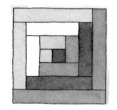

Block A   Block B

2 Arrange the blocks as illustrated in the photograph below, then sew the blocks together in rows. Press, then sew together the rows of blocks.

3 Attach white borders to the sides of the quilt top. Press, then add a white border to top and lower edges. In the same manner, attach the pink and the red borders.

4 Layer the quilt *(see page 31)*.

5 Because there are so many seam allowances, Log Cabin designs usually are either quilted in-the-ditch or echo-quilted 0.75 cm away from the seams. Quilt around the blocks in long continuous lines up, down and across the quilt.

6 Trim the backing and wadding to 1.25cm beyond the red on all sides. Insert permanent basting just within the seam. Add the binding with a 0.75 cm seam, to finish 2 cm wide. Date and sign your quilt.

Log Cabin Variations

By changing the block arrangements, hundreds of different quilt designs emerge. The following are the best-known examples. The Barn Raising pattern (see page 76) is identified by light and dark concentric diamonds. When the dark halves and the light halves are placed together, a pattern of dark and light diamond shapes appears, giving us the pattern Light and Dark Variation (see page 75). When every alternate block is reversed, a design of dark and light diagonals emerges to create the pattern Straight Furrows (right). Such patterns as Courthouse Steps (below right), Chevron Log Cabin and Pineapple (see page 79) are constructed by changing the arrangement of dark and light strips in the individual block.

Above: *Straight Furrows Log Cabin Variation* quilt

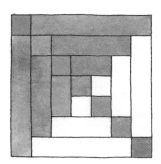

Chimney variation

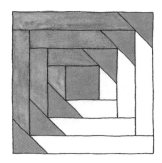

Cobwebs in the Cabin

Left: *Courthouse Steps Log Cabin Variation* quilt

Pineapple Log Cabin Quilt

Skill level Intermediate
Finished size 159 x 139.5 cm
Block size 19 x 19 cm
Number of blocks 56

Materials

- ♦ 1.9 m backing, 150 cm wide
- ♦ 1 single-bed-size wadding (optional)
- ♦ 2.75 m white novelty weave
- ♦ 70–100 cm red/cream print
- ♦ 7.8 m mixed red/white print
- ♦ 25 cm red solid
- ♦ 2.6 m lightweight calico or thin paper for the foundation
- ♦ Matching sewing threads

Cutting

Calico or paper

♦ Enlarge the template on page 174. Cut 56 squares, each 21cm, and mark the foundation grid on each.

Red solid

♦ Cut 56 squares, each 5.5 cm.

White novelty weave

♦ Cut the fabric into strips, each 3.5 cm wide, for logs.

Main red/cream print

♦ Cut strips 8 cm wide to total 6.2 m for binding and to finish 3.25 cm wide.

♦ Cut remainder into strips 3.5 cm wide for logs.

Mixed red/white print

♦ Cut 56 assorted strips, 36 x 4.75 cm wide, for corner strips on blocks (one strip is enough for one block).

♦ Cut the remaining fabric into strips 3.5 cm wide for logs.

Sewing

1 Pin the centre red square to the foundation. Sew white strips to opposite sides of the centre as shown below.

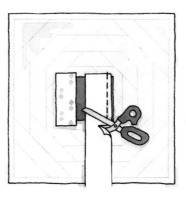

2 Press, then sew strips to top and bottom of the centre square *(see drawing at top of next column)*.

3 Change to red print strips, placing them diagonally across the corners of the previous strips with the seam just touching the corners of the red centre *(see drawing at top of next column)*. Again working opposite sides, attach the strips, press and trim as you go. Try to use the same fabrics on the round; however, there is no need to use the same fabric in the same place in each block.

4 Trim away the excess fabric from the previous round of white strips.

5 Proceed in the same way with the next round of white, again having the seam just touching the corners of the first white round. Press and trim excess fabric from the previous round.

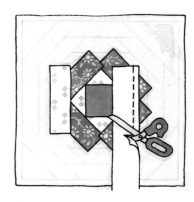

6 Continue adding red print and white print rounds alternately.

7 The true pineapple pattern appears when subsequent seams no longer coincide with those of previous rounds.

8 When no more white strips can be added, use the 4.75 cm-wide strip of red print to complete the four corners of the block.

9 Work 56 blocks in this way. If working over paper foundations, tear the paper away before continuing to the next step.

10 Arrange the blocks in seven rows of eight blocks and sew together into rows. Join the rows to complete the top.

11 Centre the top on the backing and baste together.

Finishing

1 Tie the layers together at the block corners as invisibly as possible on the front, using matching thread. Alternatively, machine-quilt the main block seams.

2 Secure the edges with permanent basting within the 0.75 cm seam allowance. Trim the backing fabric to 2.5 cm larger than the edge of the quilt on all sides.

3 Bind the quilt following the instructions on page 171. Sign and date your quilt to finish.

Curved Piecing

....

This Double Wedding Ring design presents two challenges: one is the accurate piecing needed for the arcs of the rings, and the second is the successful working of the curved seams required for assembling it. Machine paper-foundation piecing is the key to the first, while easing answers the second. Easing is the fitting together of two apparently opposing curves.

The instructions below will help with assembling any curved-seam design, such as Fans, Snail Trail or New York Beauty.

If you have tried the foundation method described for string piecing, you will notice a difference when sewing curves – the tracing paper is on top and the fabric is underneath.

MAKING A SAMPLE BLOCK

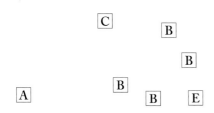

Quarter *Double Wedding Ring* block

1 Using the pattern provided on page 175, make templates for the

background pieces A and C, adding a 0.75 cm seam on all sides. Make eight tracings of the B ring unit. The solid line indicates the stitch line. Add a 0.75 cm seam on all sides.

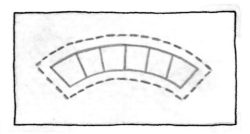

2 To piece the B units, cut 6.5 cm-wide strips from different-coloured scrap fabrics.

3 Place unit B foundation paper drawn side down. Centre the first fabric strip, right side up, over one end and trim to a rough rectangle. Pin or hold in position with a dab of fabric glue.

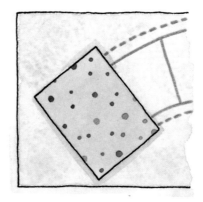

4 Put the second piece of fabric over the first, right sides together, and pin to hold in place *(see drawing at top of next column).*

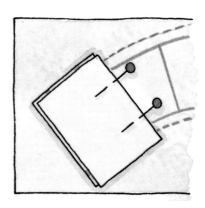

5 Turn the work over so that the paper tracing is on top. Sew along the drawn stitching line into the seam allowances at the beginning and end.

6 Turn the tracing fabric side up. Trim seam allowance to 0.75 cm. Flip the second piece right side up and finger-press in place. Pin or hold with a dab of glue *(see drawing next page).* Repeat until the tracing is covered with fabric. Make seven more units in the same way. Press and trim both the fabric and the tracing to the marked seam allowance.

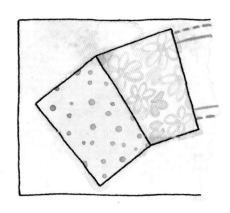

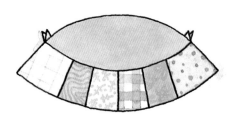

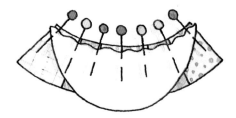

7 Cut one A and four C patterns from the background fabric. Cut eight corner squares (E), four from light fabrics and four from dark fabrics, each 5.25 cm.

Easing curved seams

8 Put a pieced B unit with a C piece right sides together. With raw edges level, match the centre and the ends. Carefully pin together at right angles to the sewing line, easing the fullness equally in the spaces between the pins. The pins should be inserted exactly 0.75 cm from the raw edges. This is your sewing line.

9 With the B unit on top, sew the two units together. Fold right sides over and press carefully. Repeat to make four more units *(see drawing at top of next column)*.

To Complete the Block

10 Add a dark E square to both ends of two B units and a light E square to each end of the remaining two units.

11 Sew one of these units to the strip completed in steps 3–7 to make four elliptical D units. Ease the curves together just as before, now also matching the corner of the E squares to the junction of the C piece and the B unit. Press.

12 Mark the 0.75 cm seam with a pencil dot on the wrong side of the A pieces at the four points. Do not sew beyond the dot.

13 Place the A piece right side up and fit the D units with light E squares top and bottom and the other D units to each side. Sew each ellipse to piece A. Remove the tracings from the B units once stitched in place.

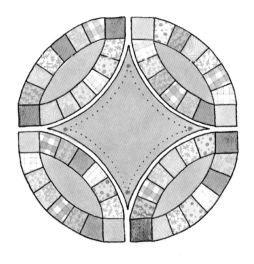

Above: The finished block

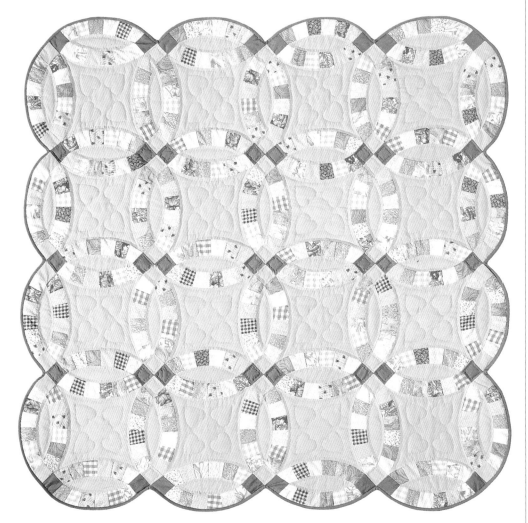

To assemble a *Double Wedding Ring* quilt like this, work eight circular blocks and set them with eight elliptical D units and eight A pieces.

Left: *Double Wedding Ring* quilt

Miniature Patchwork

·······································

Manipulating very small fabric pieces, whether cutting or sewing, presents even the most experienced quilters with difficulties. Stitching over a foundation marked with design lines eliminates many of the problems inherent in working on a small scale and achieves accurate results quickly. Accurate measuring and cutting is not necessary, as the pieces are trimmed after sewing. Use a machine straight stitch over a paper foundation and then tear away the paper or use a calico base and sew by hand or machine. The calico remains behind the block and acts as a stabiliser. To be consistent, all border areas should be backed with the same weight of calico.

MAKING A SAMPLE MINIATURE BLOCK

1 Onto paper, accurately trace the tree block design lines with a well-sharpened embroidery transfer crayon *(see page 174 for templates).*

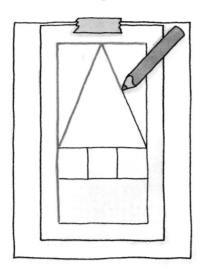

2 Place the tracing face down in the centre of the foundation. Use a hot iron to transfer the design to the fabric. Several prints can be made from one tracing.

3 Each shape on the template is numbered, and the pieces must be sewn in numerical order. For the trunk, select an appropriately-coloured scrap of fabric 0.75 cm larger all around than the trunk shape. Place

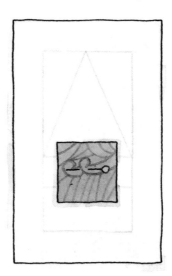

the scrap right side up on the unmarked side of the foundation. Hold the block up to the light to help position the fabric correctly. Pin and baste in place.

4 For piece 2, cut a scrap of sky slightly larger than the template and position it right side down on top of the trunk. Align the raw edges, then pin and baste in position.

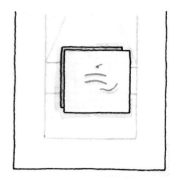

5 Flip the block over to the printed side. Sew on the printed line, joining piece 1 to piece 2: start and finish stitching just beyond the ends of the printed lines. If machine sewing, choose a shorter stitch length (1.75–2 mm) than for usual piecing.

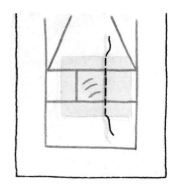

6 Turn the block over and trim away the excess seam allowance. Press the pieces flat. Continue to trim and press after each step.

7 In the same way, attach a second scrap of sky fabric to the opposite side of the trunk. Continue adding pieces in the sequence marked on the template. Ensure that all the pieces on the outer edges of the block are large enough for a 0.75 cm seam allowance around the outside.

PROJECT

Little Seaside Town Wall Hanging

Little Seaside Town Wall Hanging

Skill level Intermediate

Finished size 44.5 x 44.5 cm

Materials

♦ One fat quarter metre for backing
♦ 50 cm calico for block and border foundations
♦ One fat quarter metre for the border
♦ One fat eighth metre for the binding
♦ Scraps for houses, trees, beach huts, schooners and sky *(see templates, pages 174–175)*. (Hand-dyed fabrics make attractive skies. Small stripes and checks work well for bricks and timber. Details, such as chimneys, doors and window frames, can be worked with novelty fabrics or embroidered onto the finished block by hand or machine.)
♦ Embroidery transfer crayon and greaseproof paper
♦ Tiny sea shells and beads for embellishment
♦ Sewing threads

Cutting

Calico
♦ For the foundation blocks, cut three pieces, each 10.5 x 13 cm, for the schooners; 10 squares, each 10.5 cm, for houses and beach huts; and four rectangles, each 10.5 x 6.5 cm, for the trees. Put the remaining calico to one side and cut the borders when the quilt centre is complete.

Sewing

1 Following steps 1–5 on page 82, mark and sew the blocks.

2 Arrange six houses and four trees into two rows, then the four beach huts and three schooners into separate rows. Stitch the blocks into four rows using a 0.75 cm seam.

3 Cut 2.75 cm-wide border strips from border fabric and calico. Baste calico to wrong side of printed border. (The border is now the same weight as the pieced foundation.) Treating them as one piece, add border to the sides of the centre panel. Press, then attach to the top and bottom.

4 Cut 6 cm-wide strips for the outer border. Back with calico as in step 3, then add to the sides, top and bottom.

Finishing

1 Spread out the backing right side down and centre the quilt on top. Baste the layers together, then machine quilt the sky, ground and sea in a random manner. Stitch a single line of echo-quilting 0.75 cm outside the inner border.

2 Bind the quilt, using strips cut 3 cm wide, to give a finished 0.75-cm binding *(see page 171)*.

3 Machine zigzag around the windows and door to represent window and door frames. Add tiny beads for doorknobs and scatter seashells around the inner border and below the beach huts.

String Piecing

Strings are long, narrow strips of fabric of varying widths, often remnants or scraps from dressmaking or quilting projects. The strings are sewn together to make up a pieced fabric that has the random and asymmetrical appearance of Crazy patchwork. Anyone who likes the thrifty aspect of patchwork should enjoy this technique, as should quilt makers who are skilled in exploiting the improvisational aspect of working with a random mix of colour and pattern.

Where possible, use similar weight fabrics for the strings and a compatible foundation fabric. Remember to wash all fabrics, including the strings, before sewing. Protect them from fraying by placing them in a mesh bag.

MAKING A SAMPLE

1 Collect a mix of fabric strings. Make your own strings from straight fabric strips by cutting down their length at various angles.

2 Any of a variety of foundations, such as thin calico, can be used. The foundation remains permanently behind the strings. Lightweight paper, thin non-iron interfacing, or tearaway stabiliser can also be used. These are torn away after sewing. For a non-fabric foundation, use a short stitch length on the sewing machine.

3 Mark the foundation with the shape you wish to cover. It should be larger than the template so that it accommodates take-up during sewing. (A machine-piecing template with a 0.75 cm seam is provided on page 176.)

4 Place one string on the foundation right side up, aligning the raw edge with that of the foundation. The string should extend beyond the drawn shape at both ends. Pin to hold. Place a second string on top of the first, aligning raw edges and right side down. Pin, then stitch through all three layers, using 0.75cm seam.

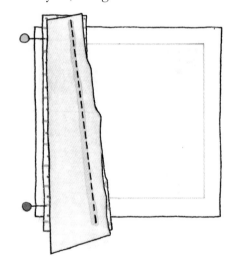

5 Grade the seam allowance to reduce the bulk, then open the second strip and press.

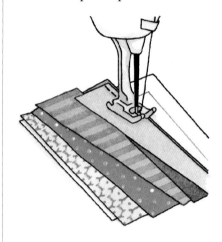

6 Continue to add strings until the foundation shape is covered. Press the pieced fabric.

7 Place your template right side up on the right side of the pieced fabric. Draw around it with a fabric marker, then cut out the shape carefully. If using a paper foundation, remove it after cutting.

String Stars Quilt

Skill level Intermediate
Finished size 174 x 212 cm
Finished block size 38 x 38 cm
Number of blocks 20

Materials

♦ 1.9 m calico for backing, 2.3 m wide
♦ 1 double-bed-size wadding
♦ 2.3 m red
♦ 1 m gold
♦ Mixed strings, equivalent to 2.2 m area when pieced, for making string-pieced diamonds
♦ 40 cm plaid for 1-cm binding
♦ 2.3 m foundation
♦ Matching sewing and quilting thread

Cutting

♦ Make a machine-piecing template for the star point using the diamond pattern on page 176. On the foundation fabric mark 160 diamonds.

Red
♦ Cut 80 squares, each 12.5 cm, for block corners.

♦ Cut 20 squares, each 19.5 cm, and divide diagonally both ways for block side triangles.

♦ Cut 16 setting squares, each 6.5 cm.

Gold
♦ Cut 36 strips, each 39.5 x 6.5 cm, for the setting strips.

Contrast plaid
♦ Cut seven strips 4 cm wide x the full width of the fabric for 1 cm binding.

Sewing

1 Follow the instructions on page 85 and string-piece 160 star points.

2 Arrange the points in sets of eight.

3 Lay out the blocks with red corner squares and side triangles, following insetting instructions on page 64 and eight-seam joins on page 70.

4 Lay out and assemble the blocks, gold setting strips and red squares. The setting strips and squares are along one long edge only *(see photograph)*.

5 Mark the quilt with concentric arcs. Cut a strip of template plastic 25.5 x 2.5 cm. Make holes down the length at intervals. Fasten one end to a point on the right side of the quilt top with a pin, then put a pencil in each hole in turn and swing to draw the arcs. Repeat over the quilt, swinging the arcs to meet the previously marked set.

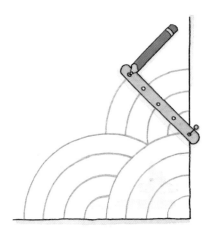

6 Assemble the quilt layers and quilt. Bind the edges of the quilt to finish 1 cm wide *(see page 171)*.

Crazy Patchwork

Crazy patchwork peaked in popularity in the latter half of the nineteenth century. The name refers to the irregular and random manner in which these quilts are pieced. Traditional crazy quilts often feature recognisable patchwork blocks, such as Log Cabin or Fans, as if included as practice pieces. Worked over a foundation fabric, crazy quilts are scrap quilts in origin; they are traditionally made with scraps of exotic fabrics like velvet, silk and brocade. By nature bright, colourful and lavish, crazy quilts are embellished with ribbons, lace, 'found' objects, beads, small pictures and embroidery. Shisha mirrors and sequins are modern additions.

The accompanying quilt project on page 90, inspired by the church of St. Eustache in Les Halles, Paris, is a modern interpretation of crazy patchwork and, unusual for this type of patchwork, contains wadding. The quilt is worked as 25 separate units that are applied to a black ground.

MAKING A SAMPLE BLOCK

1 Assemble a wide selection of textured fabric scraps, such as velvets, silks and brocades. Collect an assortment of hand embroidery threads and objects to embellish the quilt surface, such as shisha mirrors, beads and ribbons.

2 Cut a foundation square of calico larger all around than the finished project to allow for take-up.

3 Begin in the centre working outwards *(fig. 1)*, or at the corner and work across the foundation block *(fig. 2)*. Position strips of fabric right side up and overlap by 1.5 cm. Pin in place. Work with the shapes as they are and trim the excess.

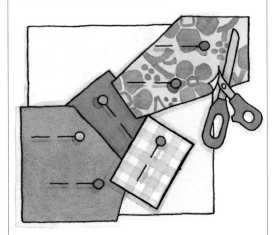

fig. 1

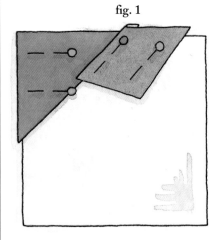

fig. 2

4 Turn under 0.75 cm along the overlapped edges and blind-hem in position. Either work a piece at a time or position a few pieces, turning them under and basting as necessary; then blind-hem the group *(see drawing at top of next column)*.

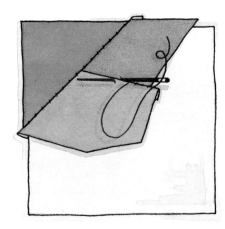

5 When the foundation square is covered with patches, work decorative embroidery stitches over the seams. Embroider additional motifs as desired.

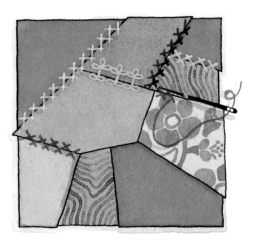

HELPFUL HINT

♦ Crazy borders for quilts can be assembled in the same way as the crazy quilt top, by adding assorted patches to long foundation strips.

Early twentieth-century *English Crazy Quilt*

Chatelet Quilt

Skill level Advanced
Finished size 157.5 x 157.5 cm

Materials

♦ 1 double-bed-size wadding (charcoal colour if possible)
♦ 7.1 m black
♦ 1.9 m calico for foundations
♦ 2.3 m approximately of mixed rich fabric scraps, such as silks, satins, brocades and metallics
♦ 25 gm purple chunky chenille yarn
♦ Assorted hand-embroidery threads
♦ Assorted embellishments, such as beads, sequins and shisha mirrors
♦ Black machine and quilting thread

Cutting

♦ Make templates of the window shapes *(see page 176)*. Make a full-size paper template of the whole design and cut out the window shapes.

♦ From calico, cut 12 squares, each 29.5 cm, for the hearts; 12 rectangles, 32 x 16 cm, for the wedges and one square, 30.5 cm, for the circle. Mark a heart template in each 29.5 cm square. Repeat for wedges and circle.

♦ Divide the black fabric into two lengths, each 167.5 cm long, and two lengths 172.5 cm long. Place each pair right sides together and sew along the selvage, using a 2 cm seam. Trim away the selvage and press the seam open. The smaller piece is for the quilt top (centre the seam horizontally), and the larger piece is for the backing (centre the seam vertically).

Sewing

1 Fill each shape with crazy patchwork. All the shapes incorporate light- and pale-coloured fabrics to resemble a stained-glass window. Extend the patchwork filling 0.75 cm beyond the outline of each shape. Replace the template to ensure that the whole area has been filled in, as the foundation can become distorted during sewing. Add any embroidery or other embellishments at this stage while the shapes are small enough to handle with ease.

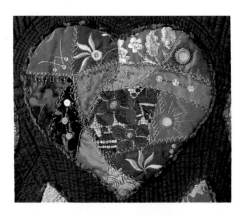

Detail of embellishment

Detail of embroidery

2 Trim the foundation to include 0.75-cm turnings. Turn under and baste the seam allowance.

3 Centre the full-size paper pattern on the right side of the black fabric and mark the window positions through the cut-out shapes.

4 Position each of the crazy-pieced shapes on each marked window. Pin, baste, then blind-hem in position. Couch purple chenille yarn around the outline of each shape.

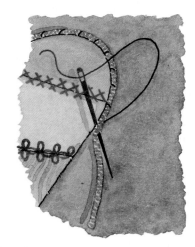

Finishing

1 Assemble the three quilt layers *(see page 31)*. Outline-quilt the window shapes. Fill the rest of the top with radiating lines of quilting.

2 Trim the quilt top to measure 157.5 x 157.5 cm, ensuring the corners are square. Trim the wadding to the same size. Trim the backing to be 2.75 cm larger on all sides. Fold the backing over to the front. Turn under 0.75 cm around the raw edge of the backing and blind-hem in position. Add a hanging sleeve. Sign and date to finish.

Chatelet Quilt

Hexagons

This method, although old, is still an accurate way to hand piece tessellating designs. Hexagonal, or honeycomb, designs are traditionally worked over paper or cardboard templates that are removed as the units are sewn together.

Fabric hexagons are cut 0.75 cm larger all around than the paper template, and the excess fabric is folded over the template and basted to secure. The basting is worked through all the layers, including the template.

The equal-sided hexagon is the most popular shape and appears in countless versions of Grandmother's Flower Garden. Elongated variations, such as the Church Window and the Coffin shape, appear in nineteenth-century English quilts and bedcovers.

Today paper templates are sometimes replaced by a lining of interfacing. Iron-on interfacing stays in the finished work.

PIECING HEXAGONS OVER PAPERS

1 Make a master template without seam allowances from plastic and use this to cut one template *(use the pattern below)* from stiff paper for each hexagon (old greeting cards are ideal).

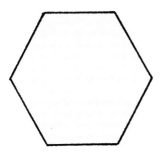

2 Place the template on the wrong side of the fabric. Mark and cut a fabric hexagon with a 0.75 cm seam allowance all around.

3 Fold the seam allowance over the template, finger-press, and baste in place as shown below. Prepare all hexagons in this way. For speed and greater ease, small pieces of masking tape can be used to hold the seam allowances in place.

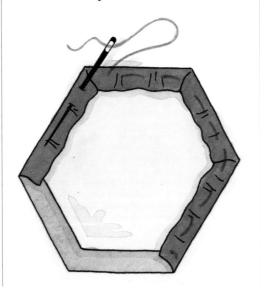

JOINING HEXAGONS

1 To join two hexagons, place right sides together with all sides even. Choose a sewing thread that blends with all the fabrics being stitched and whipstitch just into the edge of the fabrics where they are folded over the papers without catching the template. Make your stitches small and even. Secure the thread at the end with a couple of stitches.

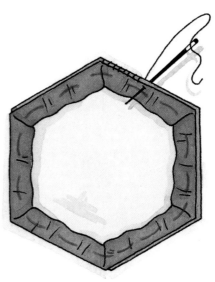

2 Where possible, move on to an adjacent seam, picking up the next hexagon and holding it in place, right sides together, against an already stitched hexagon.

3 Remove the basting threads and the templates after sewing together several hexagons. For support, keep the papers in place along the outside edges. Remove them on completion of the project.

Detail of early nineteenth-century *English Flower Basket*, pieced with 4 cm hexagons

Clamshells

The tessellating curved shape of the clamshell is ideal for piecing over papers. Here, skill lies in getting smooth curves as well as fitting the shapes together accurately to give a neat appearance.

MAKING SAMPLE CLAMSHELLS

1 From plastic, make a master template of the shell pattern below without seam allowances.

2 Use the template to cut freezer-paper shapes, also without seam allowances.

3 Working on an ironing board, place a scrap of pressed fabric

right side down and place a freezer-paper shape, waxy side down, onto it. Iron so the freezer paper adheres to the fabric. Let cool before handling.

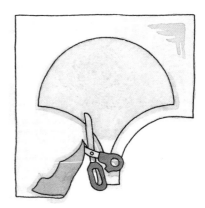

4 Cut out around the shape, adding a 0.75cm turning on all sides by eye *(see drawing at top of next column)*.

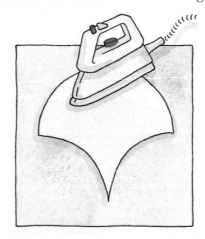

Clamshell template

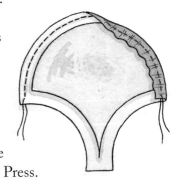

Hand sewing

5 To prepare the shells by hand, fold the excess around the top curve over the freezer-paper edge and baste in place through all layers. The seam allowance around the bottom two concave curves does not have to be turned in. To machine sew, set the machine to a large stitch and reduce the top tension. Sew around the top curve within the seam allowance. Shells can be chained, but leave tails of thread between each. Tighten one of the threads to gather the seam allowance into a snug-fitting curve over the freezer paper. Press.

Machine sewing

6 Cut a strip of paper 60 x 10 cm. Draw a straight line across the centre. With the paper on a flat surface, arrange several clamshells, right side up, along the line so that they overlap by just their seam allowances. Pin or baste to the paper.

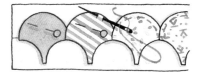

7 Position a second row of shells in the arcs formed between the first row. Baste to the paper foundation around the top curves.

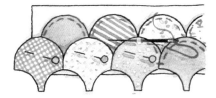

8 Blind-hem the second row to the first. Traditionally, this step is worked by hand, but when prepared this way, it can be machine stitched with invisible monofilament thread.

9 Remove the paper strip. Position a third row of shells, pinning or basting their top edges to the seam allowances of the previous row.

10 Continue to build up the project, removing papers as rows are sewn, except at the outside edges. Remove these when the work is complete.

Detail of 1920s *Clamshell* quilt made with scrap fabrics

Cathedral Windows

Cathedral Windows projects are not true quilts in that they usually have no filling, but they are one of a group of novelty techniques that have identified themselves more closely with quilting than with any other sewing discipline.

The technique involves folding and refolding squares and stitching each together to give the appearance of windows. It is a deceptively simple technique and can be readily enjoyed by a needlework novice – a large square is folded to frame a smaller, contrasting-colour square and can be sewn successfully by hand.

MAKING A SAMPLE WINDOW

1 Cut two squares, each 16.75 cm, of background fabric. Cut one 5 cm square of accent fabric for the window.

2 Lightly mark the centre of a 16.75 cm square by folding along both diagonals and creasing lightly with the point of the iron. Turn under 0.75 cm on all sides to the wrong side.

3 Fold each corner into the centre to make a block, 10.5 cm. Using a needle and knotted thread, secure the corners in the centre with a small cross-stitch. Do not cut the thread.

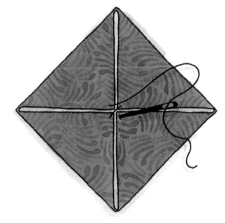

4 Press, then fold the corners in again to the centre point, press, and secure with a cross-stitch. The side with the folds is the right side of the square. Repeat steps 2–4 for the second 16.75 cm square.

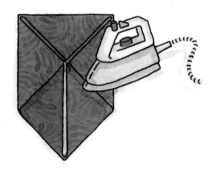

5 Place two prepared squares right sides together and overcast with an invisible stitch along one edge. Do not pull the stitching too tightly. Doing so will make a ridge that prevents the pieces from lying flat.

6 Place a 5 cm square on-point over the seam between the two joined squares. Trim until 0.25 cm of background is visible all around. Pin in place.

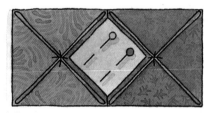

7 Turn the bias folds of the background over the edges of the window square and stitch in place, stretching them into a smooth curve as you go. Blind-hem or use a tiny spaced backstitch. Do not pull the stitching too tight – a pinched look will spoil the finished appearance of your work.

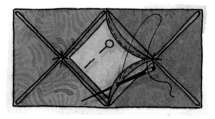

8 To finish the corners securely, bring the two folds close together with a tiny bar-stitch about 0.75 cm from the point to ensure that the raw edges of the window fabric underneath are completely covered.

Bar stitch

Secret Garden Unit

This simple-to-sew unit makes four neat petals. Combine it with the basic unit for more variety and flexibility of design.

1 Cut one square, 16.75 cm, for the background and one window square, 7.75 cm.

2 Prepare the background square following the instructions in steps 2 and 3 on page 96. Cut the thread.

3 Fold the four corners to the centre again and press but do not stitch. Open out and check that the fold lines are clearly visible. If not, refold. Centre the accent square on-point inside the folds. Trim if required. Secure the square with a small permanent running stitch close to the raw edges.

Detail of *Secret Garden* units used in the quilt project on page 98

4 Refold the corners to the centre. Press and secure in the centre with a cross-stitch.

5 Turn the pairs of bias folds away from each other to reveal the accent fabric beneath and sew neatly in place *(see drawing in next column).*

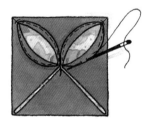

6 Make a bar stitch to hold the folds together 0.75 cm from the corner *(see drawing at top of first column).* Repeat with all four pairs of folds to make the four petals.

7 To add greater variety and colour to your Secret Garden units, make several different pieced *four-patch* accent squares.

Cathedral Windows Silk Wall Hanging

Skill level Intermediate
Finished size 81.25 x 106.75 cm
Number of Cathedral Window background squares 78
Number of Secret Garden units 30

Materials

Plan A indicates the colour and placement of background squares. The shaded squares represent the Secret Garden units. Plan B indicates the window colours and the Secret Garden accent fabrics.

♦ Iron lightweight interfacing to the wrong side of very delicate silks.

Background-fabric squares
♦ 40 cm grey-mauve print (**A**)
♦ 40 cm magenta (**B**)
♦ 25 cm solid lilac cotton (**C**)
♦ 40 cm pink suede print (**D**)
♦ 40 cm purple print (**E**)
♦ 40 cm red-violet print (**F**)
♦ 60 cm pink-lilac print (**G**)
♦ 25 cm purple solid (**H**)
♦ 40 cm aubergine (**J**)
♦ 60 cm lilac and green (**K**)
♦ 25 cm green (**L**)
♦ 25 cm violet print (**M**)
♦ 1.9 m violet solid (**N**)

Borders and windows
♦ 70 cm pink shot silk (**O**)

Windows
♦ 20 cm rose shot silk (**P**)
♦ 20 cm old rose (**Q**)
♦ 20 cm blue silk (**R**)

♦ 70 cm wadding
♦ Matching threads

Plan A

A	A	B	B	C	D	E	A	A
E	H	G	G	C	F	D	E	A
G	H	G	N	J	F	D	D	B
B	B	N	K	J	F	F	F	B
B	N	J	K	J	J	J	D	B
N	K	K	L	K	K	D	E	M
A	N	N	K	J	F	D	E	M
G	G	N	K	J	F	D	C	G
G	G	N	K	J	D	E	C	G
H	H	N	K	D	E	E	M	M
A	E	B	N	H	G	C	G	M
A	A	M	H	G	G	C	A	A

Plan B

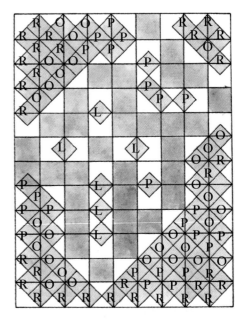

Cutting

Background fabrics
♦ For the backing, from fabric **N** cut one rectangle, 117 x 90.5 cm. Cut a strip 82 x 23 cm for the hanging sleeve.

♦ Cut a total of 108 squares, each 16.75 cm, as follows:
From fabric **A** x 11.
From **B** x eight.
From **C** x six.
From **D** x 11 for the Secret Garden variation.
From **E** x nine.
From **F** x seven.
From **G** x 14.
From **H** x six.
From **J** x nine for the Secret Garden variation.
From **K** x 10.
From **L** x one.
From **M** x six.
From **N** x 10 for the Secret Garden variation.

Window fabrics
♦ Cut a total of 93 squares, each 5 cm, as follows:
From **L** x six.
From **P** x 25.
From **R** x 32.
From **O** x 30.

Lining for Secret Garden
♦ From **K** cut 11 squares, each 7.75 cm.
From **Q** cut 11 squares, each 7.75 cm.

Borders
♦ From pink **O** cut two strips 12 x 109.75 cm and two strips 12 x 87 cm. (Measurements include 1.5 cm seams.)

Sewing

1 For the Secret Garden variations, line each **D** square with a **Q** square following steps 3–5 of the instructions on page 97. Line each **N** square with a **K** square. Note that not all the folds are opened out and stitched. The **J** squares do not have a window square. Stitch back the bias folds.

2 Following Plan A, prepare all the background squares as directed in the instructions on page 96. Arrange each square according to the quilt layout.

3 Hand sew the background squares into pairs beginning at the top-left corner.

4 Add the window squares over the seams as coded on Plan B.

5 Assemble into fours, always working methodically across the quilt following the plan. Use the photograph of the wall hanging to see which folds are stitched.

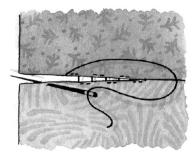

Ladder stitch

6 Add the Secret Garden units as you come to them *(see page 97)*.

Finishing

1 Cut four strips of wadding to fit the border strips. Wadding is used in the borders to balance the many layers in the quilt centre. Machine stitch a strip of wadding to the wrong side of each border along the side that will be attached to the quilt top, 1 cm from the edge. Trim the wadding close to the stitching within the seam allowance.

2 Find the centre of one short border strip and match to the midpoint of the lower edge of the quilt top,

overlapping the strip by 1.5 cm. Pin and baste in position. Blind-hem the edge of the quilt top to the border.

3 Repeat with the top border. Then add the sides in the same way, mitring each corner *(see page 168)*.

4 Press the backing fabric and place right side down with the quilt top, right side up, over it. Baste through all the layers.

5 Tie the layers *(see page 165)* as desired, with the tails at the back. Quilt the border in-the-ditch.

6 Trim the wadding to 1.5 cm smaller all around than the border.

7 Make a fold-finish around the outside edge, turning over 1.5 cm of the backing to enclose the wadding. Baste the two without coming through to the front of the work. This stitching will remain in place. Complete as directed for fold-finishing on page 171.

8 Make and attach a hanging sleeve *(see page 35)*.

9 Sign and date the back of your work to finish *(see page 167)*.

Biscuit Patchwork

....

Also known as puff patchwork, this technique is ideal for projects for babies and young children. They are warm, lightweight, very easy to make, and well suited to being made with fabric scraps.

Each biscuit is made by sewing together two similarly shaped but different-size units. The larger, top shape creates a small baggy pocket that is then lightly filled with a loose stuffing. When the biscuit is closed the stuffing traps the air giving it a three-dimensional quality.

MAKING FOUR SAMPLE BISCUITS

1 Press all the fabrics before cutting, as once assembled, the biscuits are not easy to press. From calico, cut four 9.25 cm squares for the base. Cut four 11 cm squares of the top fabric.

2 Pin one large square right side up over a calico square, with the top-right-hand corners matching.

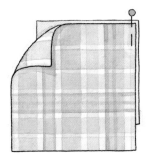

3 Now match the top-left-hand corners and pin in place *(see drawing at top of next column)*.

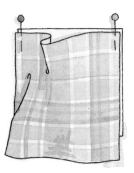

4 Make a small pleat at both ends of the top seam, about 1 cm from the raw edges, so that the larger square fits the base square. Pin the pleats.

5 If hand sewing, sew the two layers together with matching thread and within the 0.75cm seam, securing the pleats and making new ones on both sides of all corners. Leave an opening along the middle of one side large enough to insert the filling when all sides have been sewn.

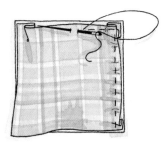

6 If machine sewing, form pleats on both sides of all corners and pin before stitching. With a scant 0.75 cm seam allowance, start sewing just before one corner and stop just after the fourth corner to leave an opening to insert the filling.

7 Prepare all four biscuits in the same way and fill with wadding.

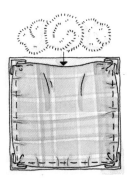

8 Sew the filled biscuits together in pairs, placing the open edge of one to a seamed edge of the next. Sew a full 0.75cm seam to make sure the previous stitching is covered. The seam allowances can be lightly pressed with just the point of the iron along the turnings to avoid crushing the filling. Then stitch the pairs together.

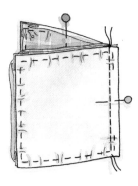

Yo-yo Patchwork

....

Yo-yos are single circles of fabric gathered up to produce three-dimensional fabric shapes. Yo-yos can be stitched together into lacy fabrics, or they can be used to embellish stitched or pieced surfaces. Lightweight cotton fabrics with a tight weave that do not fray easily are ideal for this type of patchwork.

MAKING A YO-YO

1 To make a small yo-yo, cut a 7.75 cm circle of fabric.

2 Thread a needle with a length of cotton and knot one end. Sew a running stitch around the outer edge of the circle, turning under a small seam to the wrong side as you work.

3 Gather up the running stitches, pulling the thread tightly. Secure with a small stitch and trim the ends.

4 To make yo-yo fabric, sew yo-yos together into rows with neat overcast stitches.

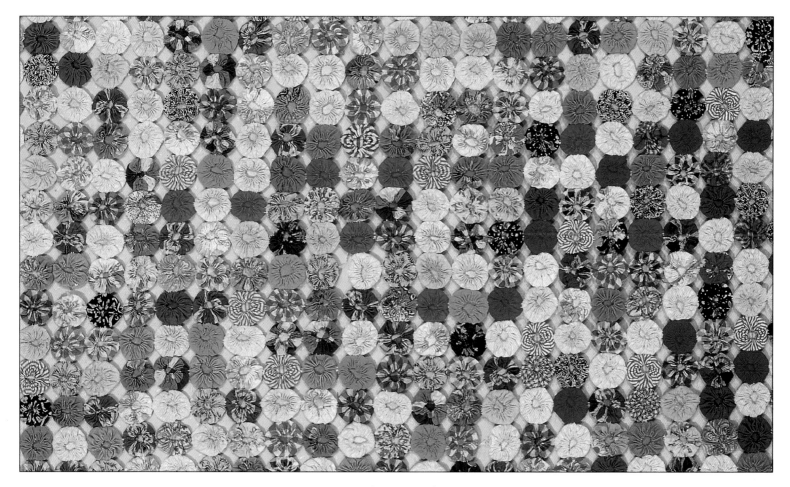

1950s *Yo-yo* quilt

Representational Patchwork

Pieced blocks are most commonly associated with abstract geometric patterns. However, there are a number of representational designs that remain firm favourites with quilters. These include Maple Leaf, variations of the Pine Tree design, Sailboat and numerous Basket designs. Many subjects lend themselves to simplification into basic geometric components and, with a skilful combination of straight lines and curved piecing, new designs can be created.

Opposite are a few examples of inventive use of piecing. There are no hard-and-fast rules of representing objects in patchwork, because much depends on the quilter's skill in translating the design into a workable unit and the amount of detail needed for a realistic representation. Successful patterns are those that translate easily into geometric shapes. The accompanying project on page 104 uses a variation of the popular Schoolhouse design.

DESIGNING A REPRESENTATIONAL BLOCK

1 Choose an image for your representational block. Use two

L-shaped framing strips made of cardboard to help you identify the parts of the image you want to use.

2 Place tracing paper over the image and, with a pencil and a ruler, trace the main shapes. Curves can be drawn in freehand at this stage.

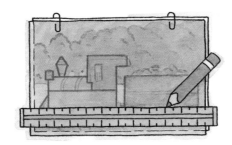

3 From the tracing, decide on the most suitable block shape for the motif, such as square, square on-point and square with sashing strips.

4 Draw the block outline onto graph paper. Transfer the image, maintaining the proportions of the parts into the block outline. Tidy freehand drawn curves with compasses or a flexible curve.

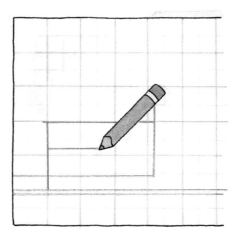

5 Study the design to determine how to sew it most efficiently. Look for awkward inset corners or very sharp angles. If necessary, add extra seams or continue existing seams to the edge of the block *(see the drawing below)*. Then use fabric pattern or colour to help conceal these essential construction lines.

Consider using the flip-and-sew method *(see page 82 in Foundation Piecing)* for sewing small shapes and sharp angles.

6 Return to your original picture to identify which remaining details are needed to complete the representation effectively. Some shapes that are too awkward for piecing may be appliquéd. Other details can be embroidered.

7 Make a paper pattern and sew a test block from scrap fabrics. When the block is successful, ink in the pattern with a fine-line marker to make the master design.

Above: *Hens*. This sturdy hen uses strips sewn into *Log Cabin* blocks.
Half-square triangles in two sizes make the head and tail feathers.

Above: *Maple Leaf*. The stylised simplicity of the leaf is achieved with
speed-pieced half-square triangles.

Above: *Pine Tree*. The block is set on-point, and the branches are made
of strips following the method for joining strips on page 116.

Above: *Sailboat*. The hull of the boat is a rectangle with half-square
triangles at each end. The sails are all made from half-square triangles.

Above: *Aeroplane*. The aeroplane block is pieced with five simple shapes.
The propeller is appliquéd.

Schoolhouse Quilt

Skill level Intermediate
Finished size 91.5 x 119.5 cm
Block size 23 x 23 cm
Number of blocks 12

Materials

♦ 1.4 m backing and sleeve
♦ 1.2 m wadding, 150 cm wide
♦ 50 cm unbleached calico
♦ Scraps at least 8 x 50 cm each of 12 different plaids
♦ 60 cm navy for setting strips
♦ Scraps, minimum 13 x 26 cm of garnet red, ginger and earthy red for setting squares
♦ 25 cm yellow for outer border
♦ 25 cm red plaid for binding
♦ Matching sewing thread and embroidery threads for tying

Cutting

Navy
♦ Cut eight strips, each 6.5 cm wide, across the width of the fabric. From these, cut 31 strips, each 24.5 cm long.

Yellow
♦ Cut five strips, 2.75 cm wide, across the width of the fabric. From two of these, cut strips 96.75 cm long for top and bottom outer borders. Divide a third strip in half. Trim the selvages from the two remaining strips; then to each strip add half of the third strip. Trim to 122.25 cm long for side outer borders.

Red plaid
♦ Cut strips 4.5 cm wide across the width of the cloth and 4.5 m long in total for 0.75 cm double binding.

Setting squares
♦ Cut scraps into 6.5 cm wide strips, then cross-cut into 20 squares total, each 6.5 cm, in a mixture of colours.

Unbleached calico
♦ Cut 10 strips, each 4 cm wide, across the width of the fabric. From these cut 12 strips 48.75 cm long (**A, B, C, D**); 12 strips 16.75 cm (**M**); 12 strips 9.25 cm (**O**) and 24 strips 5.25 cm (**F**) long.

♦ Cut 12 rectangles, each 6 x 8 cm. To make triangles for the roof section, divide six rectangles diagonally top left to bottom right (this will make 12 for the right-hand end of the block – **J**). Divide the remaining six from bottom left to top right to make 12 triangles for the left-hand end (**K**).

♦ Cut 12 strips, each 3.5 x 13 cm (**I**), to divide the roof gable from the side.

Each schoolhouse plaid
♦ Cut two strips, each 4 x 48.75 cm (**A, B, C, D**). Divide one strip into lengths of 25.5 (**C, D**), 14.25 (**G**) and 9 cm (**E**).

♦ Cut a rectangle 6.5 x 19.5 cm for the side of the roof (**H**). Mark 5 cm from the lower-left-hand corner along the bottom and from the top-right-hand corner along the top. Cut from the appropriate corner to the mark to make the required parallelogram.

♦ Cut a rectangle 7 x 10.5 cm (**L**). Mark the midpoint of one long side. With a rotary cutter and a ruler, cut from opposite corners to the midpoint mark to make the roof gable.

♦ Cut two pieces, each 4 x 5.25 cm, for the chimneys (**N**).

Making One Schoolhouse Block

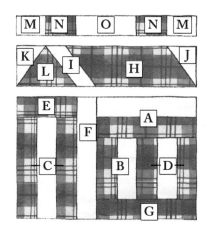

1 With right sides together, sew the 48.75 cm plaid to a matching calico. Press seam towards plaid. Cut one length 14.25 cm for the top of window (**A**) and one 9 cm for the vertical (**B**).

2 To the calico side of the remaining strip add the 25.5 cm plaid. Cut one 14.25 cm strip (**C**), one 9 cm (**D**).

3 To one short side of the **C** piece sew a plaid 9 cm strip (**E**) to make the top of the doorway. Press open, then add a calico strip 16.75 cm (**F**) long to the right-hand side.

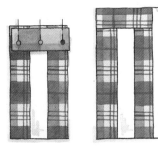

4 Sew pieced units **B** and **D** together, keeping the sequence correct for the window. Sew a plaid 14.25 cm strip (**G**) to the lower edge. Press, then add the **A** unit to the top *(see drawing on the next page)*.

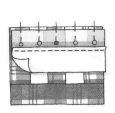
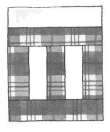

5 Sew the window unit to the right-hand side of the door unit.

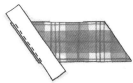

6 Pin the 3.5 cm-wide calico strip (**I**) on one of the short parallelogram (**H**) sides and sew. After pressing, trim the excess calico level top and bottom.

7 Sew triangle **J** to the other end, positioning it carefully with 0.75 cm points extended beyond the roof edge.

8 Stitch the remaining calico triangle **K** to the left side of the roof gable (**L**). Press, then sew the gable to the roof side.

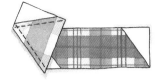

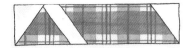

9 Alternate the remaining 4 cm-wide strips of calico (**M**) and plaid (**N**) at each side of the calico 9.25 cm strip (**O**) and seam together. Assemble the chimney, roof and house together.

Finishing

1 Make 11 more schoolhouse blocks. Arrange the blocks into four rows of three blocks. Sew the rows of blocks together with navy setting strips.

2 Sew five horizontal setting units by alternating four contrast setting squares and three navy strips. Join the rows of blocks and setting units.

3 Attach a long yellow outer border to the two sides of the quilt, trimming as necessary. Then add the remaining yellow strips to the top and bottom, trimming accordingly.

4 Layer the quilt *(see page 31)* and in the centre of the blocks and setting squares use three colours of embroidery thread to tie the quilt *(see page 165)*, trimming tails to approximately 1.5 cm.

5 Finish with 0.75 cm red plaid binding *(see page 171)*. Add a sleeve for hanging *(see page 35)*. Sign and date your quilt to finish.

Colour-wash Patchwork

....

Colour-wash patchwork refers to the technique of piecing together small squares of printed fabric to create shaded abstract designs. The technique is influenced by the Impressionist paintings in which colours and values change almost imperceptibly across the surface of the work. The impression of form is created by the pattern size and subtle blend of colours. A concentration of colour at the centre of the design, diffusing outwards and emphasised by patterns of increasing size, creates depth and proportion. For this lesson, I have chosen an exercise in grading and arranging fabric squares. When selecting fabrics, avoid ginghams, stripes and polka dots (mini-dots may be suitable), as these designs are often too distinctive to blend together satisfactorily.

PRACTISING THE COLOUR-WASH TECHNIQUE

1 Choose a wide range of printed fabrics in varying colours, hues and pattern sizes. From each, cut squares 5 or 7.5 cm. Smaller squares may not offer enough of a pattern, while larger squares may provide too much of one colour or pattern, so that it dominates. Use the wrong side of a print fabric to yield a softer shade.

2 Sort the squares by colour, then by tonal value (light, medium and dark) within each colour family. Use the colour wheel to help blend the colours. To help sort out the colour

values, put anything not read instantly as light or dark into the medium pile. Divide the medium selection again into medium-light and medium-dark.

Light   Medium   Dark

3 Next, choose swatches from two colour ranges. Arrange one set of squares in a column from dark to light and the second set from light to dark, blending the two together in the centre so that the medium colours diffuse into each other. Repeat the same exercise using just one colour and differing values. The aim is to create a unit block in which the fabric swatches all blend with each other without jarring or drawing attention to any one square. Be prepared to discard any squares that prove too eye-catching. Finally, arrange blocks of different colours or values to create contrasts between blocks.

4 A reducing glass identifies any errors in position, but using the viewfinder of a camera or the wrong end of a pair of binoculars works equally well. Look through red cellophane or a red plastic viewer to more easily detect errors in value placement of your fabric selection.

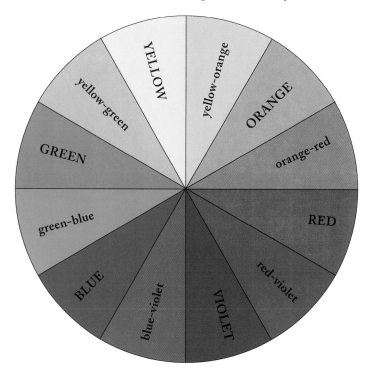

Colour-wash Stripes with White Triangles

Vase of Flowers Wall Hanging

Skill level Beginner / Intermediate
Finished size 81.25 x 71 cm

Materials

◆ 1 m backing
◆ 1 m wadding
◆ 25 cm turquoise for binding
◆ 50 cm space-dyed turquoise for inner and outer borders and vase
◆ 50 cm peach print for first background and middle border
◆ 25 cm peach-cream print for second background
◆ 25 cm peach-turquoise for the tablecloth
◆ Scraps of three prints showing sprigs of flowers for the outer sprays of flowers on light peach or cream grounds
◆ Scraps of seven densely packed small floral prints, each with different background colours
◆ Cream sewing thread
◆ Peach and light turquoise quilting thread

Cutting

Space-dyed turquoise
◆ For the inner border, cut two strips 2.75 x 71.5 cm and two 2.75 x 61.5 cm. For the outer border, cut two strips 6.5 x 89.5 cm and two 6.5 x 79.5 cm.

◆ For the vase, cut a 5.5 cm-wide strip from the width of the fabric, and cross-cut into 14 squares, each 5.5 cm.

Turquoise binding
◆ Cut strips 3 cm wide totalling 3.5 m for the binding to finish 0.75 cm.

Peach
◆ For the middle border, cut two strips, each 5.5 x 76.5 cm, and two strips, each 5.5 x 66.5 cm.

Peach and Peach-cream background print
◆ From both fabrics, cut 86 squares, each 5.5 cm. (It is not necessary to have equal numbers of both prints.)

Peach-turquoise print
◆ For the tablecloth cut 28 squares, each 5.5 cm.

Outer floral sprays
◆ Cut 29 squares, each 5.5 cm, focusing on the printed sprigs.

Floral prints
◆ Cut 81 squares, each 5.5 cm, from the seven different prints. Use the chart on the next page as a guide.

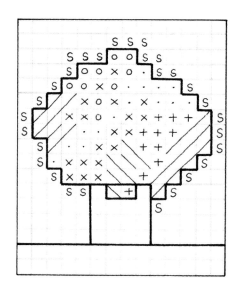

Key for Colour-wash

- S Floral prints on cream grounds
- ⟋ Blue/turquoise ground and flowers
- O Red ground blue/mauve flowers
- x Red ground, red/orange/turquoise flowers
- · Smallest flowers brown, cream, orange, turquoise
- ⟍ Magenta ground
- + Dark blue ground, red flowers

Sewing

1 Arrange the 28 peach-turquoise squares for the tablecloth.

2 Assemble the vase. Use the back of some of the squares to suggest a lighter side of the vase.

3 Fill in the background squares, arranging the two fabrics in a chequerboard design.

4 Use the chart as a guide to position each of the flower sprays. The final arrangement will depend on the choice of fabrics. The deeper colours were placed low in the arrangement, and the fabric with the smallest flowers was sprinkled diagonally across, creating an illusion of airiness and light. Stand back and review the composition. Be prepared to rearrange squares and discard some. Use the back of the fabric to aid transition from one area to another.

5 Sew the squares together in rows, using 0.75 cm seam allowances. Press the turnings in opposite directions on adjacent rows before sewing the rows together to complete the centre panel. This will ensure that the seams interlock *(see page 29)*.

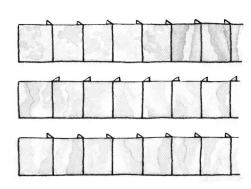

6 To assemble the border strips into four sets, first find the centres of all strips. Match the centres of adjacent strips when sewing the peach middle border between the two turquoise strips, again with 0.75 cm seams, so that the sets will already be shorter on the inside ends for the mitres.

7 To attach the borders, match the midpoint of the sides of the centre panel to the midpoints of the

borders and sew accurately 0.75 cm from the end at both start and finish on each side. Fold and sew the mitres as directed on page 168.

Finishing

1 The flowers were quilted with a petal-like design similar to the traditional wineglass pattern. This should be marked on the quilt top in the flower spray only.

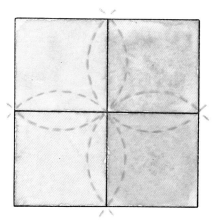

2 Assemble the quilt layers *(see page 31)*, pin, and baste.

3 Work the marked quilting design. Add horizontal quilting lines across the tablecloth and diagonals across the background as if radiating outwards from the centre. Quilt in-the-ditch around the borders.

4 Prepare the edges with a row of permanent basting, then add 0.75 cm binding with automatic mitres *(see page 171)*. Sign and date. Add a hanging sleeve to finish *(see page 35)*.

Fragmentation

....

Fragmentation refers to the division of patchwork blocks into smaller units. Adding more pieces to the design allows greater interplay of shape, colour and tone, creating a sense of movement and adding visual interest. For accurate construction, this technique demands competence in the piecing and assembling of basic units, an understanding of colour and a strong sense of design.

For the lesson, use the Four Card Trick block as the whole quilt top and fragment it using straight seams. Then consider ways to fragment the background. Fragmentation is most successful when the eye perceives an overall unity. Symmetrical designs need not always be fragmented in the same way throughout.

FRAGMENTING A BLOCK

1 On paper, draw the various components of the block; divide the blocks in the following way:

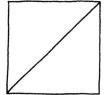 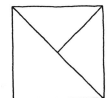

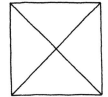

2 Sub-divide the units in different ways. Experiment by leaving parts of the original design undivided or by fragmenting the whole unit.

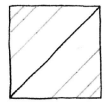 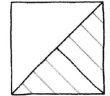

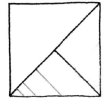 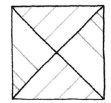

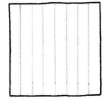 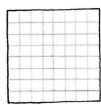

3 Interpret these designs using fabric scraps or colouring pencils. Experiment with colour and hue,

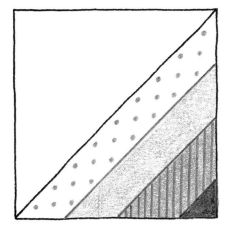

making subtle changes by altering the basic colour by degrees of light and dark. For example, grade from the darkest shades in the centre to lighter shades at the outer edges. Alternatively, use contrasting colours to create a dramatic effect, as in the centre of the unit below.

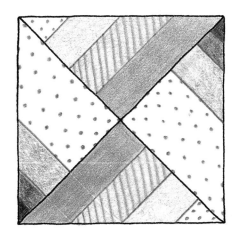

4 From these experiments, choose those fragmentations that work best together and colour in the whole design.

Four Card Trick Block

Flower Power Quilt

Flower Power Quilt

Skill level Advanced
Finished size 198 x 198 cm
Block size 20 x 20 cm
Number of blocks 81

Materials

♦ 1 double-bed-size wadding
♦ 2.1 m backing, 2.3 m wide
♦ 1.6 m black
♦ Mixed pastel prints on a light ground equivalent to 2.3 m
♦ Mixed colourful medium prints equivalent to 2.3 m
♦ Mixed dark prints on a black ground equivalent to 3.2 m
♦ Graph paper, cardboard or template plastic

Cutting

Templates
♦ Make 20 cm templates for patterns 1–4.

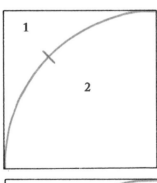

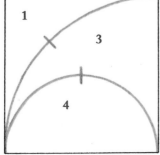

♦ On graph paper, draw two squares, each 20 cm. In each square draw a grid of four rows of four squares. Divide each block into its component parts by drawing the curved lines on the grid. Cut out the shapes.

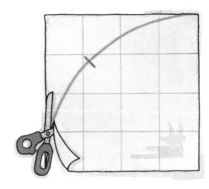

♦ To understand the piecing of each curve, attach each shape to a 20 cm square of cardboard and continue the grid squares on the cardboard to complete the squares. These grids show

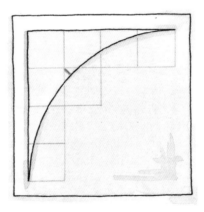

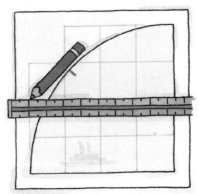

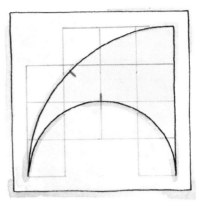

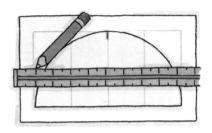

the configuration of pieces to be sewn, and on which the templates fit.

Black
♦ From the width of the fabric, cut eight strips, 9 cm wide, for the borders.

♦ From the width of the fabric, cut eight strips, 5 cm wide, joining them together to make continuous binding.

♦ Using template 1 and adding seam allowances, cut eight shapes; cut one shape using template 3; and cut three shapes using template 4.

Mixed prints, all values
♦ Cut strips 6.5 cm wide from all fabrics and cross-cut into 6.5 cm squares. Separate the three values.

Sewing

1 The quilt top is pieced together in nine sections of nine blocks each.

Key

■ Solid black

■ Dark prints

▨ Medium prints

☐ Pastel prints

This keeps the units manageable but of a scale sufficient to ensure that the colours of each block flow easily into the next. Use the key as a guide to the correct position of each tonal value.

2 For each configuration in turn, sew together pieces of the correct value. Press the seams.

3 Using the templates, cut each shape from the relevant pieced unit, adding seam allowances and marking centre points.

4 Arrange nine blocks in each group. There should be a harmonious transition of colour between blocks.

5 Sew the curved shapes together into single blocks, using a 0.75 cm seam allowance, following the directions for

curved seams *(see Curved-seam Piecing, page 68)*.

6 Sew the blocks into rows of three, then stitch the three rows together to complete each section.

7 To make sure that the colours of one section flow into or contrast with the next, keep completed sections together when arranging the colour scheme of the remaining blocks. A design board would be useful here.

8 Stitch together the nine sections.

Finishing

1 Join the border strips lengthwise, two for each side of the top. Then attach each border to the quilt top,

using either butted or mitred corners *(see page 168)*.

2 Layer, pin, and baste the quilt top, wadding and backing. Protect the edges by folding over excess backing.

3 Hand or machine quilt the design, following the curves of the motifs.

4 Add a line of permanent basting within the seam allowance around the edges. Trim the wadding and backing 0.75 cm larger than the top.

5 Add the binding, sewing 1.25 cm from the trimmed edge, then fold over and blind-hem into place to finish 1.25 cm wide.

6 Sign and date your quilt to finish *(see page 167)*.

Optical-illusion Patchwork

....

From the mid-nineteenth century, optical-illusion quilts have developed into an art form. With no formal training in geometry or colour, some quilters chose to make quilts that challenged the normal perceptions of a simple bedcover, creating quilts that artistically preceded their generation by at least a hundred years.

Optical-illusion quilts cause the eye to see a three-dimensional shape while the mind recognises the flat surface of the quilt. By manipulating colour, shape and line, by placing light and dark blocks in juxtaposition to each other, quilters create receding or advancing images, a sense of movement, increasing or decreasing space and layers of design.

Traditional patterns, such as Tumbling Blocks, Log Cabin variations and Kaleidoscope, give the illusion of three dimensions. Other illusions exist. With transparency, the mind sees layers of colour that appear to pass in front of or behind each other. With vibration solid complementary or contrasting colours of the same value are placed side by side repeatedly to dazzle the eye.

DESIGNING A THREE-DIMENSIONAL GRID

1 On isometric graph paper, imagine a light shining at one corner of the paper. Using a light-value pencil, colour in all the diamonds that face towards the light. The shapes on the opposite side, away from the imagined light, should be coloured with a dark

colour. The remaining diamonds should be coloured with a medium-value pencil.

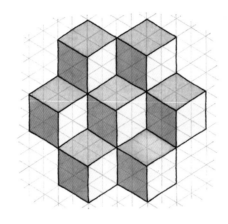

Above: Tumbling block designs drawn on isometric graph paper

TRANSPARENCY

1 To demonstrate the effect of transparency, cut two triangles from different-colour transparent material, such as cellophane or chiffon. Overlay one triangle over the other at different angles. At the point of overlap, a third colour appears *(see page 115, fig.1)*. This is transparency in its simplest form.

2 The more difficult aspect of transparency is in the translation of illusion into pieced fabric. In the *Ohio Star* quilt opposite, one large *Ohio Star* block appears to float over a

background of small Ohio Star blocks. The large star appears to stand independent of its background and at the same time to merge with it. The effect is created by the use of two predominant colour schemes. Light and bright shades of pink and yellow are used in the large star, while hues of black, navy, and grey merge to form a dark background. The overall unity of the design is retained by the muted colours that cause the large star of the foreground to blend into the background. The large star design is a reflection of the smaller stars – the repetition draws the design together.

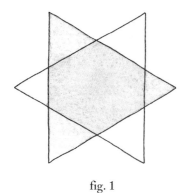

fig. 1

VIBRATION

1 The exercise is to understand how colours interact and make each other seem to vibrate. Using the colour wheel on page 106, collect bright, solid-colour paper samples of the same value, choosing colours from all parts of the colour spectrum. Choose one colour and place it on top of the other colours in turn to study the effect. Maximum vibration occurs between identical values of two colours exactly opposite each other on the colour wheel.

Left: *Cuilfail Spiral*

Above right: *Ohio Star*

Right: *Kipper Ties*

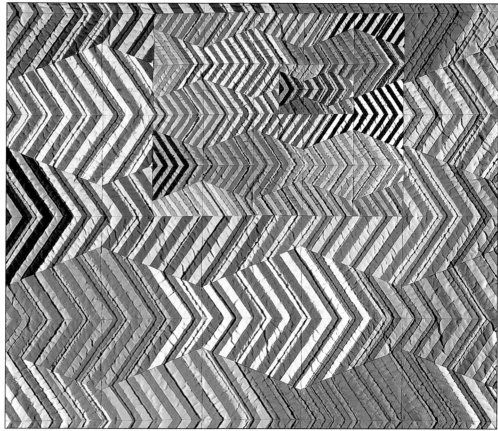

Black-and-White Optical-illusion Quilt

Skill level Advanced
Finished size 200 x 185 cm

Materials

♦ 2.2 m backing, 2 m wide
♦ 1 double-bed-size wadding
♦ 3 m black
♦ 2.3 m total solid white and a variety of white-on-white (patterned) fabrics
♦ 1 m striped fabric for binding
♦ Matching sewing and quilting thread

Cutting

Black
♦ Cut eight strips, each 14 cm wide, across the width of the fabric and set aside for borders.

♦ Cut strips 7.75 cm wide x the width of the fabric. Cut more as required.

White
♦ Across the width of the fabric, cut strips from the solid white 7.75 cm wide. Cut more as required.

♦ Cut strips of different widths from the white-on-white fabrics.

Striped fabric
♦ Cut strips 11.5 cm wide across the width of the fabric to total 8.3 m for binding, to finish 5 cm wide.

Sewing

1 Following the instructions on page 58 for strip-piecing, stitch together the white-on-white lengths of fabric in a random manner. Press.

2 Using a quilter's rule, mark a 45° angle across the direction of the strips. Parallel to the marked line, cut diagonal strips 7.75 cm wide. Make more as required to use for the shaded white-on-white areas. Use the plan on page 191 as a placement guide.

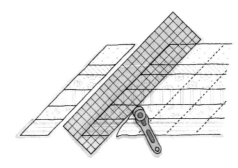

3 Above the quilt opposite is a scale, each unit measuring 6.25 cm. Where a strip changes colour diagonally, that unit must be added to both colours *(see below)*. To calculate the length of each section, count the number of units (counting twice at diagonals). Multiply this figure by 6.25 cm, then add 1.5 cm for seams.

4 For example, for the left-hand side of the top strip, cut two 7.75 cm squares from the 7.75 cm-wide black strips, and one 51.5 cm strip. From solid white, cut two 20.25 cm strips. Arrange each in the correct sequence.

5 Stitch one horizontal strip at a time. The sections are joined at a 45° angle, as for continuous binding. Finger-press a diagonal on one black square. Place with the 20.25 cm white strip, right sides together, aligning short

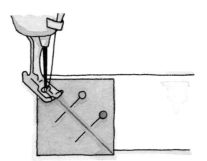

fig. 1

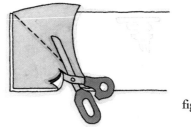

fig. 2

raw edges. Pin, then stitch across the diagonal fold, ensuring the seam slopes in the correct direction *(fig. 1)*.

Trim away the excess fabric and press *(fig. 2)*. Place the second black strip at the other end of the white strip, right sides together and at a right angle to it. Stitch across the diagonal *(fig. 3)*.

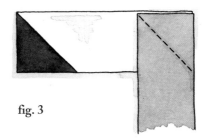

fig. 3

6 Continue to stitch one strip at a time, including the patterned strip-pieced whites. Check all strips following the quilt plan before joining each together to complete the top.

7 Join the 14 cm-wide strips as necessary to make the borders. Sew to the sides, top and bottom of the quilt *(see page 168)*.

8 Layer, pin, and baste. Echo-quilt inside the squares and triangles fabric at 5 cm intervals. Quilt remaining background with a single line along the middle of the strip.

9 Prepare the edges with a row of permanent basting just inside the 0.75 cm turning. Trim the edges of the backing and wadding to 4.25 cm larger than the quilt top.

10 Join the striped binding and attach to the quilt with a 0.75 cm seam. Fold over to the back, turn in 0.75 cm and sew to the machine stitching, to finish 5 cm wide.

Below: The scale divides the strips into square units and is used to calculate the length of each section. It may help to extend the scale on a sheet of clear plastic placed over the photograph.

6.25 cm units

APPLIQUÉ

Appliqué is simply a technique of stitching fabric shapes onto a background to create a design. It can also be used to repair damaged or worn clothing. Its appeal lies in the infinite variety of designs possible.

The technique dates back to the ancient Egyptians, and examples can be found in early European and Asian needlework. Popular during the medieval period, appliqué was used to decorate clothing, military banners, ecclesiastical robes, bed hangings and household furniture.

Appliqué is often considered a more luxurious associate of patchwork. The appliqué quilt was once thought to be a 'best quilt', one to be brought out only on special occasions. As a result, appliqué quilts have fared better than their utilitarian counterparts, and many magnificent examples survive as a testament to the skill and artistry of nineteenth-century needlewomen.

Appliqué has many guises, including broderie perse, reverse appliqué, stained glass and shadow appliqué. Most can be applied either by hand or by machine with an invisible blind-hem stitch or decorative embroidery stitches, such as buttonhole or satin stitch. It is an expressive technique that allows considerable freedom in design and execution.

Left: Detail of nineteenth-century *Album Quilt*

A Library of Appliqué Blocks

....

Although the pictorial nature of appliqué invites any motif as a suitable subject, the most popular motif traditionally has been the flower. In the nineteenth century, during the heyday of fine appliqué quilts, flowers appear in bouquets, wreaths, sprays, urns, baskets, vases and garlands, and as single blooms. The ubiquitous rose appears in numerous guises – from the biblical (Rose of Sharon) to the political (Whig Rose).

During the appliqué revival of the 1920s, the market was flooded with new commercial designs that often reflected the popular culture of the time, such as Sunbonnet Sue, Bronco Buster, Colonial Lady and a variety of figures from nursery rhymes. Still, despite the pictorial innovation in available patterns, floral designs continue to be the most popular subject for appliqué design.

Frequently seen combinations of hearts, birds and potted flowers reflect a strong link to folk-art motifs from the areas known today as southern Germany, Austria and Switzerland, and it is not too fanciful to imagine a link between their folded paper-cut designs and the appliqué designs used by the Pennsylvania Dutch quilters. The four-way and eight-way symmetry of folded-paper designs are a feature of nineteenth-century appliqué.

Many nineteenth-century appliqué quilts share a colour scheme of red and green on a light ground. Artistically complementary, these colours were chosen as a result of contemporary conditions – plain calico as a ground was cheap and plentiful, most vegetable dyes were unstable, and Turkey Red cloth, although expensive, was reliably colourfast and brilliant in hue.

The appliqué designs below and on the following page are just a starting point. In the tradition of the art, modify a design to please your taste or, better still, make up your own.

Cockscomb and Currant

Pinecone

Fleur de Lys

Cornucopia

Whig Rose

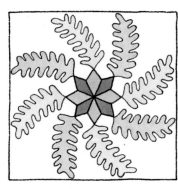

Princess Feather

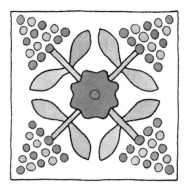

Berries

Rose Wreath

Love Apple

Patriotic Eagle

Tulip Basket

Iris

Sunbonnet Sue

Farmer Bill

Scottie Dog

Snowflake

Oak Leaf and Reel

Bluebird

Preparation for Hand Appliqué

....

Good preparation is essential to speedy and accurate appliqué. Preparation need not be limited to one method, as no one method gives more accurate results; try all methods and use those that work best for you. Finger-pressing is fast if you choose to appliqué using the needle-turning technique. Basting shapes before applying them allows for maximum control when sewing down. Card-pressing with starch is good for bold simple motifs and the shapes can be applied to the background with any hand stitch. Using freezer paper for appliqué preparation ensures a stable and crisp edge when sewing.

ENLARGING A DESIGN

The easiest way to enlarge any appliqué design is with a photocopier. However, you may prefer to enlarge the design using the grid method.

1 Make an exact drawing of the size of block you intend to use and mark with a grid of equal-size squares, each no larger than 5 cm.

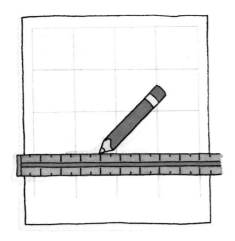

2 Draw a grid of the same number of squares over the design you wish to enlarge.

3 Copy each part of the original design onto the corresponding square of the large grid.

PREPARING THE BACKGROUND FABRIC

1 Cut blocks 2–3 cm larger to allow for take-up. The background can become distorted during sewing, particularly with elaborate designs.

2 Finger-press vertical and horizontal centre lines on the background for ease of positioning the design. For on-point designs, lightly crease the diagonals.

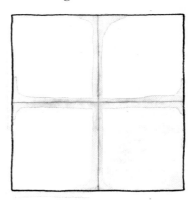

3 Mark positioning lines only; do not draw the whole design. This is time-consuming, and it can be difficult to remove markings if the appliqué drifts slightly during sewing.

4 Place the background over the master design and mark with a pencil your placement lines and points where two or more shapes overlap. Mark the linear shapes, such as basket handles, leaves and stems with a broken centre line.

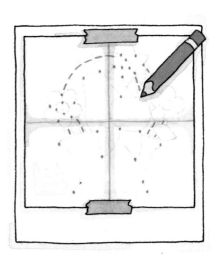

Marking and Cutting Motifs

Whenever practical, match the grain of the appliqué motif with the grain of the background fabric. This prevents motifs from puckering.

Working with light-coloured fabrics

1 Tape the design right side up on a back-lit surface, such as a light box or a window, then place the fabric right side up over it. With a well-sharpened pencil, trace the outline of the shape. The tracing line is your fold-under line. Leave a 1cm space between outlines to allow for turnings.

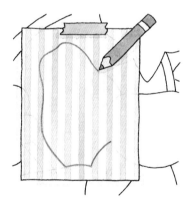

2 Cut out the shapes, adding a 0.5 cm seam allowance by eye.

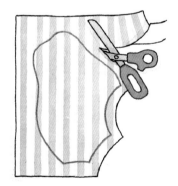

Working with dark-coloured fabrics

For dark fabrics, make a template without seam allowances. Use it to mark the outline of each shape on the right side of the fabric with either a light-coloured pencil or a sharpened sliver of soap. Cut out carefully, adding 0.5 cm seam allowance by eye.

Templates are not necessary for straight shapes, such as stems. Cut straight strips on the straight grain and press or baste the turnings in place. Curved stems must be cut on the bias, then pressed and/or basted (*see Preparing Stems on page 124*).

Preparation for Sewing

Card-pressing with starch

For this appliqué method, see the *Hearts and Hourglasses* quilt, page 33.

Finger-creasing

This is good preparation for needle-turned appliqué because the seam allowance turns under neatly along the creased line when stroked under with the point of your needle.

1 Hold an appliqué shape right side up. Fold the turning along the drawn line away from you to the wrong side and pinch to form a crease. If you are creasing in the right place, you will not be able to see the pencil line. If you can see the line on the right side of the shape, the shape will be too big. Alternatively, if the pencil line is tucked under too far, your shape will be too small for the project.

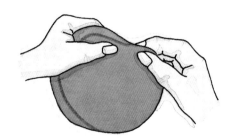

2 Don't run your fingers along as you crease or you will stretch the shape. Turn the shape as you work all the way around. Inside curves will not stay under without being snipped. Clip almost to the pencil line, but do not clip until actually sewing in place (*see step 7 on page 126*).

Basting

Basting is useful for complex appliqué designs in which the pieces must fit together exactly to prevent gaps from appearing in the work.

1 Hold the appliqué shape with the right side towards you. Fold the turning to the wrong side along the pencil line and baste in place with thread, leaving the beginning knot on the right side of the shape for easy removal later.

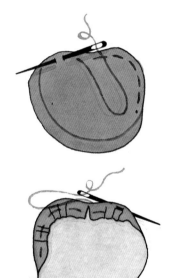

2 Edges that will be covered by another appliqué need not be basted. If necessary, snip inside curves as you reach them and space the basting stitches to hold the turnings in place. A group of basted shapes can be correctly positioned on the background fabric, then either pinned or basted before sewing in place with your chosen stitch.

Protecting Appliqué Shapes

◆ Sharp notches within shapes need to be protected. Stabilise potential weak spots with a small dab of a liquid fray preventer applied to the seam allowance. Allow to dry before proceeding.

When sewing in place, snip into the turning at the treated point; the fabric will not fray.

PREPARING STEMS

For straight stems and bias stems

Right side down, press fold along one edge.

Press the second edge to almost reach the first fold.

Prepare bias strips in the same way for curved stems.

STITCHES FOR HAND APPLIQUÉ

Running Stitch

Work the appliqué running stitch close to the turned-under edge of the shapes or 0.25 cm from raw-edge appliqué.

Whipped Variation

To make the stitching decorative, whip the running stitches attaching the motif either with the same-colour thread or with a contrast. This is a good way to emphasise the motif.

Blind-hem Stitch

When you use this stitch, the motifs appear to be held invisibly. Hold the edge of the motif towards you. Always bring the thread out in the folded edge and never on the top of the motif. The stitches must be small, even, and close together to prevent the seam allowance from unfolding or frayed threads from appearing. Avoid pulling the sewing thread too tight as this creates a pinched appearance and puckers the block.

Blanket and Buttonhole Stitches

Blanket and buttonhole stitches add definition around the outer edges of each motif. Blanket stitch can be worked in a fairly open manner on motifs with a turning pressed under and provides a decorative edging. The stitches of buttonhole stitching are worked close together to secure and protect cut edges, as in Broderie Perse. Fine, shaded embroidery thread is particularly effective for this appliqué technique.

Blanket Stitch

Long and Short Blanket Stitch

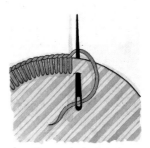

Buttonhole Stitch

Needle-turning Technique

....

Needle-turning describes how the point of the needle strokes the seam allowance on the appliqué shape to turn it under immediately before sewing. Generally, the term is associated with appliqué that looks as if the stitching is invisible because it has been worked with a very neat and inconspicuous blind-hem stitch. It is possible to needle-turn the edges and sew with other stitches, such as running and buttonhole or blanket stitch.

MAKING A SAMPLE TULIP BLOCK

1 Following directions on page 122, prepare a background square with light creases for centring the appliqué. Mark the position of the centres of the stems; use dots to indicate the points of the petals.

2 Using the tulip template on page 177, cut and prepare flower and leaf pieces by finger-creasing. For the stems, cut one strip on the straight grain, 11.5 cm long x 1.5 cm wide. Cut two strips on the bias, 6.5 x 1.5 cm. Press under a 0.5 cm seam allowance.

3 Position the curved stems, then blind-hem down both sides with matching colour thread. The raw ends that will be covered by subsequent pieces do not have to be turned under. Position the straight stem so that it covers the ends of the curved stems, trimming if necessary, then baste *(see drawing top of column 2)*.

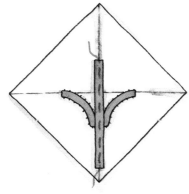

4 Pin on the first leaf, right side up, tucking one end under the basted stem. Starting on one longer side, stroke the seam allowance under with the tip of your needle as far as the pencil line and hold securely in place with your thumb.

Bring the needle up from the back of the block into the edge of the leaf and proceed to blind-hem *(see page 124)*.

Work around the whole shape, stroking under each small section before sewing. Avoid pulling the

stitches too tight, as this will crimp or pucker the fabric.

5 Work the second leaf in the same way, then blind-hem the centre stem, turning under about 0.25 cm to neaten the lower end.

6 Pin petal A to the background block and turn under the top edge only. For the point, blind-hem along one side of the pencil line right to the point. With the tip of your needle, fold under the unsewn seam allowance. Continue sewing the other side. Baste the sections that will be covered by petals B and Br.

7 Position and pin petal B following the same instructions for sewing points as described in step 6. Be sure it covers the raw edge of the centre stem. For smooth results when sewing the concave shapes, clip into the seam allowance just before sewing.

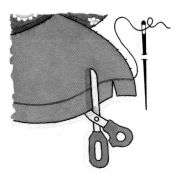

8 Finish the appliqué block by adding petal Br in the same manner. Work the two other tulip blooms in the same way.

HELPFUL HINTS

♦ To make quilting easier, trim away the background from behind appliquéd shapes. Do this very carefully, separating the two layers with a pin to avoid cutting into the motif when entering from the background fabric.

Trim, leaving a scant 0.5 cm seam allowance of background within the stitched outline. If you plan to do this, it is best done as you work. Otherwise, if you have several shapes overlapping, it will be difficult to cut away neatly and will leave you with various thicknesses behind the design.

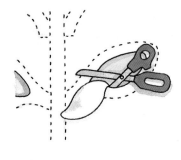

Tulips Wall Hanging

Skill level Beginner/Intermediate
Finished size 55 x 55 cm
Block size 12.75 x 12.75 cm
Number of appliqué blocks 9

Materials

♦ 70 cm calico for backing
♦ 70 cm wadding
♦ 50 cm grey-green
♦ 25 cm deep red print for binding
♦ Red and red print scraps for tulips
♦ Dark green scraps for stems and leaves

Cutting

Calico
♦ Cut a 61 cm backing square.

♦ Cut nine background squares for appliqué, each 15.5 cm. These will be trimmed to the required 14.25 cm after working the appliqué.

Grey-green
♦ Cut two squares, each 22 cm, and divide on both diagonals to make eight side triangles. Cut two squares, each 15 cm, and divide once diagonally to make four corner setting triangles.

♦ Cut four 14.25 cm setting squares.

Deep red print
♦ Cut straight-grain strips 3 cm wide and totalling 2.5 m long for binding.

Scraps of red and red print
♦ Cut 27 B petals and 27 Br petals.

♦ Cut 27 A petals.

Dark green
♦ Cut nine straight-grain strips, each 1.5 cm wide by 11.5 cm long.

♦ Cut nine bias strips, each 1.5 cm wide and 13 cm long, enough for two curved stems on one block.

♦ Cut 18 leaves.

Sewing

1 Work nine tulip blocks following the instructions on page 125.

2 Press the blocks face down over a hand towel (see page 29). Trim to 14.25 x 14.25 cm.

3 Arrange the blocks on-point with the setting squares, side triangles and corner triangles. Sew together in diagonal rows, pressing seams towards the grey-green where possible. Do not worry that the setting triangles are oversize.

4 Using the tulip template, mark the four alternating squares. Use the tulip in the side and corner triangles.

5 Assemble the quilt layers (see page 31) and baste. Work the quilting (see page 158).

6 Trim the quilt layers for a 0.75 cm finished binding. Stitch permanent basting through all layers within the seam allowance. Follow the directions on page 171 to attach the continuous binding. Make and attach a sleeve (see page 35). Sign and date your quilt to finish (see page 167).

Appliqué Using Freezer Paper

Freezer paper is a moisture- and vapour-proof product used for wrapping food for freezing. It has been adopted by quilt makers as a useful aid to appliqué. The freezer paper acts as the template, which is ironed, waxy side facing the fabric, and removed from the work before the final stitches are made. Using freezer paper eliminates the need to mark your fabric and gives a defined edge with which to turn under the fabric before sewing it down. It is not practical to use freezer paper for making stems; their narrowness would make the template very difficult to remove.

MAKING A SAMPLE ROSE AND LEAF CLUSTER BLOCK

1 Prepare a 20.5 cm background square of calico. Lightly mark the points and junctions of leaves and petals with a pencil dot.

2 From the template, trace the appliqué shapes in reverse onto the paper side of the freezer paper. Cut out the shapes on the drawn line without seam allowances.

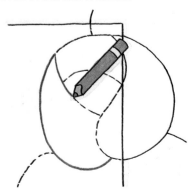

3 Iron each shape with the waxy side facing the wrong side of the fabric, spacing shapes to allow a 0.5 cm seam allowance all around. Cut out, adding the turning by eye.

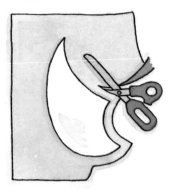

4 Position the leaves first, following the sequence marked on the template. Hold the shape in place with a pin, a tiny dab of gluestick or a couple of basting stitches. Fold the seam allowance to the wrong side and blind-hem the motif to the background *(see drawing at top of next column).*

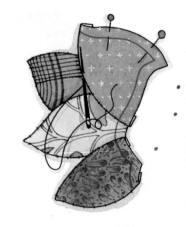

5 Remove the freezer paper just before securing the last stitches.

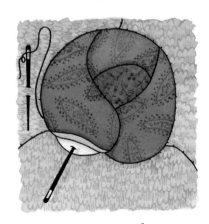

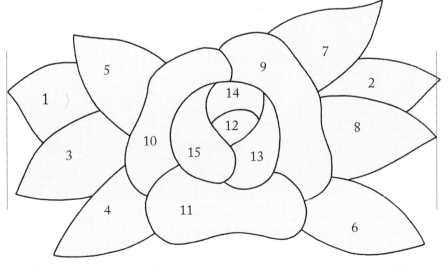

Template of *Rose and Leaf Cluster*. Enlarge to measure 17.75 cm between the two red lines.

Baltimore Basket Quilt

Skill level Advanced
Finished size 185.5 x 185.5 cm

Materials

- 4.2 m backing
- 1 double-bed-size wadding
- 3.7 m calico
- 1.9 m burgundy print
- 50 cm deep rose for the basket lining
- 40 cm burgundy/rose texture print for the basket strips
- Fat quarters for the leaves and flowers – medium and dark green prints x 9; light and medium blue prints x 8; deep rose or red prints x 4; light pinks x 5; yellow/gold/ochre prints x 4; beige on cream prints x 2; peach with green x 1; black on blue x 1
- Scraps of one turquoise print and one solid turquoise for bows
- Sewing and quilting thread
- Freezer paper

Cutting

From the patterns provided on pages 181–187, make freezer paper templates for all the motifs, remembering to trace each in reverse. Iron the shapes to the fabric, then cut out the shapes. Freezer-paper templates can be used more than once. Cut more as required. Templates are not needed for the basket strips. From cardboard or template plastic, cut templates for the basket base, body and top edge.

Calico

- Cut two outer borders, each 193 x 41 cm. These arc oversize on both length and width to allow for take-up.

- Cut two borders, each 117 x 41 cm – these are equally oversize in width as the side borders but are only 1.25 cm longer.

- Cut two inner borders 112 x 21.75 cm and two 71.5 x 21.75 cm.

- Cut the centre medallion 71.5 x 71.5 cm.

Burgundy

- Cut eight strips, 4 cm wide, across the full width of the fabric and set aside for binding to finish 1 cm wide.

- Cut five strips, 4 cm wide, across the full width of the fabric for framing.

- Using the freezer-paper template, cut the appliqué ribbon border, which consists of four corner knots, two tails, 14 straight knots and 16 ribbon swags. Cut one stretched swag later to fit the exact space available to you.

- Using templates, cut one basket base, one basket top edge and one strip 3 x 38 cm, to be pressed into thirds along its length for weaving into the basket.

- Cut some of the flowers or petals in the basket or garlands from left-over scraps.

Basket fabrics

- Using the template on page 187, cut one basket from deep rose solid.

- From the rose and burgundy print, cut 26 straight-grain strips, each 3 cm wide by 28 cm long. Press into thirds lengthwise.

Turquoise print and solid

- With templates, cut four sets of print and solid pieces for the bows.

Fat quarters for flowers, leaves, and stems

- The garland appears five times in the quilt. To make them identical, cut five of each petal, flower and leaf. Label and store each piece until needed.

- Using your freezer-paper templates, cut leaves, flowers and petals to fill the basket. You can cut all before sewing or cut a few at a time.

- To make very narrow stems, as required for the spray on the left, cut strips 2.5 cm wide and press in half.

Sewing

1 Following the instructions in Preparation for Hand Appliqué on page 122, lightly mark the 71.5 cm square for the centre medallion. Baste the basket to the background. Position and baste the vertical basket strips, beginning in the centre. Weave the

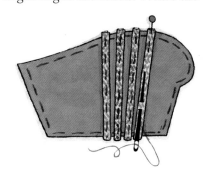

horizontal strip through the vertical strips, then blind-hem all the strips in place. Leave the sides of the horizontal strip unstitched for a more three-dimensional appearance. Add the base and top edge of the basket.

2 Fill the basket with leaves and flowers. Study the design carefully and work out your sewing sequence. Apply the underneath shapes first, then those that will be overlapped by other shapes. Remember that any parts that are overlapped should not be turned under. Remove the freezer-paper templates as you complete each shape.

3 For the narrow stems, position the strip pressed in half earlier over the stitching line so that it will be closer to the fold at the top and so that the folded fabric represents the desired finished width of stem. Sew along the stitching line using a running backstitch. Trim the excess raw edge so that it fits under the fold when the stem is flipped over. Blind-hem to the background.

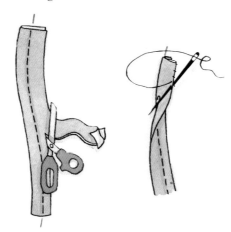

4 Trim the medallion to 70 cm square. Attach the inner-border strips with 0.75 cm seam allowances. Press the seams open. Over these work the four corner garlands. Add the turquoise bows. The medallion with borders measures 110.75 x 110.75 cm.

5 Attach the burgundy framing strips, joining as necessary to achieve the required length. The framed medallion should measure 115.75 x 115.75 cm.

6 Work the fifth garland centred on the top outer-border strip.

7 Work as much as possible of the ribbon appliqué along the two long side borders. (A corner knot at both ends and five knots connected by six swags of ribbon.)

8 Centre the top appliqué border on the top edge of the medallion and attach. Add the empty outer border to the bottom. Match the midpoint of the long side borders to the midpoint of the medallion and check that the ribbons balance on opposite sides of the quilt before sewing.

9 To complete the lower ribbon border, prepare, pin, and baste into place the remaining four knots and swags, placing them to connect with the corner knots. Measure the centre space and cut a stretched swag accordingly. Stitch this assembled lower border, then add the single rose motif.

10 Complete the ribbon border by adding the tails over the seams at the top of the quilt.

11 For the quilting mark a 1 cm grid in the medallion, and for the border parallel lines 1.25 cm apart.

Finishing

1 Divide the backing fabric into two pieces and join. Assemble the quilt layers and baste. Protect the outer edges by folding the excess backing over to enclose the wadding. Then quilt, working from the centre outwards.

2 The finished quilt should measure 185.5 x 185.5 cm, with outer borders of 36.25 cm. Insert a line of basting within the seam allowance.

3 The 4cm-wide binding should be attached with raw edges level with the quilt edge. Sew with a 1 cm seam. Fold over to the back, turn in 1 cm and blind-hem to finish 1 cm wide.

4 Make a hanging sleeve *(see page 35)*. Sign and date your quilt.

Detail of flowers in basket

Raw-edge Appliqué

As the name suggests, raw-edge appliqué shapes are applied without having the raw edges turned under. Shapes are cut out with pinking shears or with the pinking blade or wave blade of a rotary cutter. This easy method suits the skills of a beginner and is an ideal introduction to appliqué.

MAKING A SAMPLE BLOCK

1 From the patterns provided on page 177, make templates for the leaves and the robin.

2 Place each template right side down on an appropriately-coloured scrap and draw an outline. Cut out the leaves, whole body and red robin breast with pinking shears or the decorative blade of a rotary cutter; do not add seam allowances. To each wing add a 0.5 cm turning on one side to tuck under the body.

3 Cut one 15 cm square for the background.

4 Arrange the body and wings on the background, with the wings just tucked under the body on each side. Pin or baste. Sew with hand or machine running stitches 0.25 cm along the inside of the edge of each shape. Sew the wings, then the body, the breast, and the holly leaves.

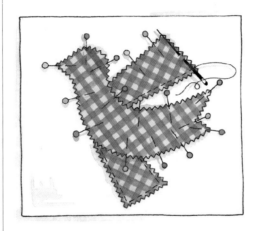

5 Embroider the bird's legs with stem stitch *(see page 138)*. Embroider the eye with a French knot.

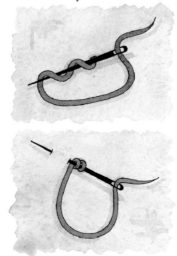

Above: Making a French knot

Right: *Skittish Robin* wall hanging

Broderie Perse

....

This appliqué technique uses motifs cut from printed fabrics, arranged into new designs, and sewn, using blind-hem stitch with a narrow turning or decorative buttonhole stitch, onto a plain background. Named because of its similarities to Persian embroidery, Broderie Perse was immensely popular during the eighteenth and early part of the nineteenth century, and probably originated with the arrival of colourfast chintzes imported from India. The fabrics enchanted the European public, who were accustomed to inferior cottons; these imports, in contrast, were exotic in colour and design. Chintzes were expensive, and when European fabric manufacturers outlawed the importing of these foreign cloths, they became harder to come by and more sought after. Hence, no scraps were too small to be used.

MAKING A SAMPLE WITH BUTTONHOLE STITCH

1 Collect a selection of printed fabrics. Home-furnishing fabrics offer a good variety of strong colour and motifs. Avoid thick fabrics, fabrics with a loose weave, linen blends and satin weaves. Cottons similar to dressweight fabrics are best. You'll also need a square of background fabric and some embroidery thread. Choose colours closest to those of the printed motif.

Right: Detail of Broderie Perse block

2 Wash and press your fabrics.

3 Working with very sharp scissors, accurately cut out your motifs. A cleanly cut edge is important. Go for bold designs for maximum effect, leaving small and intricate shapes until you are confident that you can handle them with ease. Small details, such as stems or tendrils, can always be embroidered later.

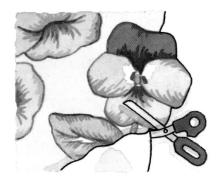

4 Arrange the motifs into a new design on the background fabric. Baste in place.

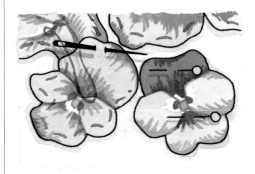

5 Work close buttonhole stitch around the outside of the shapes *(see page 124)*. When sewing around curves, use a wider stitch.

6 Remove the basting stitches. Place the work face down and press lightly *(see page 29)*.

Detail of eighteenth-century Broderie Perse bedcover with *Tree of Life* centre arrangement

Machine Appliqué Using Fusible Web

Machine appliqué is much simpler these days owing to the development of fusible-web products. When fused to fabric by the application of heat, fusible web provides stability to the appliqué motif as well as seals the edges against fraying. When fused to the wrong side of the appliqué and then to the background fabric, manufacturers claim items are secure without any further stitching. However, it is recommended that the edges of any item subject to wear, handling and washing, be machine sewn with a zigzag or satin stitch. Be sure to have the web side facing the fabric and the paper side up towards the iron or you will have a sticky mess to clean up! Protect the layers with a piece of baking parchment. Beginners to the technique should use a paper-supported fusible web. Follow the individual manufacturer's instructions. When working with delicate or heat-sensitive fabrics, protect them from the direct heat of the iron by using either paper or a pressing cloth.

MACHINE APPLIQUÉ SAMPLE USING FUSIBLE WEB

1 Cut a square of cotton fabric for the background and collect a variety of cotton scraps for the appliqué. Using the template on page 138, enlarge the shoe design to 10 cm, or larger if preferred.

2 Because the web will be fixed to the wrong side of the appliqué motifs, the pattern must be traced in reverse. To do this easily, turn the pattern over and ink in the lines on the back of the paper. Label this side 'working side'. Place the fusible web with its paper side up over the working side of the design and in pencil trace around each part of the design separately.

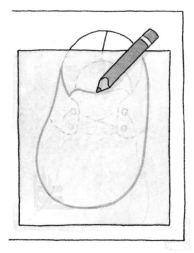

3 Cut out each piece without seam allowances.

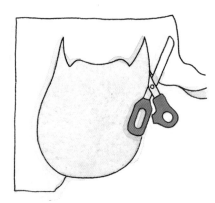

4 With an iron set on cotton, fuse each webbing shape to the wrong side of the fabric with the paper side up. Allow the pieces to become thoroughly cool before handling.

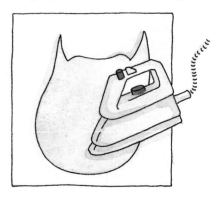

5 Cut out each of the pieces without seam allowances.

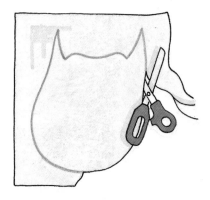

6 With the background block right side up, position all the pieces,

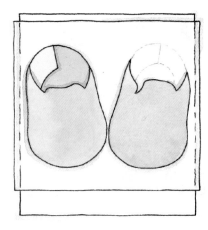

peeling away the paper backing and placing them right side up. There should be no gaps between the component parts. When all the shapes are in place, use a hot iron to carefully bond the motifs to the background block.

7 Work machine zigzag or satin stitch around the shapes, choosing matching thread or some of the shaded or variegated threads available. Work a stitch test, as the tension may need to be set slightly looser than for regular sewing.

Avoid setting the stitch length too close together, as the stitching may bunch up.

When sewing curves, guide the fabric so that the machine sews without stopping; this prevents layers of stitches from piling up.

PROJECT

First Steps Baby Quilt

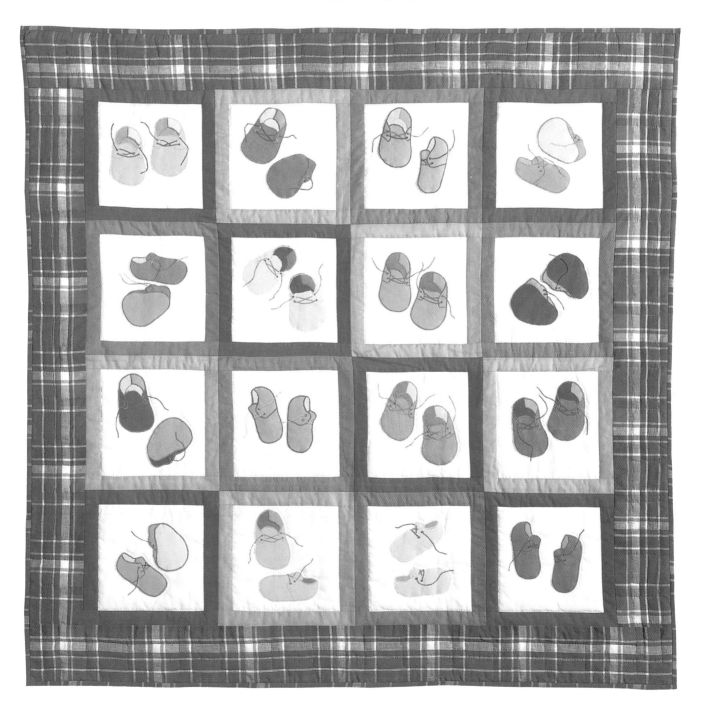

First Steps Baby Quilt

Skill level Beginner
Finished size 117 x 117 cm
Size of finished block 19 x 19 cm
Number of blocks 16

Materials

♦ 1.4 m backing, 150 cm wide
♦ 1.4 m wadding, 150 cm wide
♦ 1 m pale cream
♦ 1.3 m plaid
♦ 50 cm of three colours for framing
♦ 25 cm yellow, deep peach, pale lime, turquoise, blue-violet, pink, peach and apple-green
♦ Matching sewing, machine embroidery and quilting thread
♦ 1 m fusible web

Cutting

Pale cream
♦ Cut 16 squares, each 20.5 cm.

Plaid
♦ Cut two borders 117 x 11.5 cm and two borders 98 x 11.5 cm.

♦ From the remainder, cut straight strips 3 cm wide to total 4.8 m when joined for binding.

Bright solids
♦ Cut 16 sets of block framing strips 4 cm wide from your 50 cm colours. A set needs two strips 20.5 cm long and two strips 25.5 cm long.

♦ The appliqués will be cut as the blocks are worked.

Sewing

1 Work 16 appliqué blocks in the manner described on page 136. Use the main Baby Shoes template below right and combine it with the upside-down shoe and the sideways shoe in the Templates chapter on page 179, to create your own designs. Embroider the laces with machine satin stitch or stem stitch by hand. Chain stitch the eyelets.

2 Sew the shorter framing strips to opposite sides of the blocks first, then add the longer strips to the top and bottom.

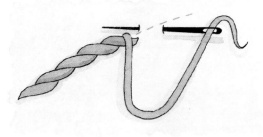

Stem Stitch

Chain Stitch

3 Arrange the blocks in four rows of four. Sew together into rows and then into one panel.

4 Add the shorter plaid border strips to the sides, then add the long strips top and bottom.

5 Layer and baste *(see page 31)*.

Finishing

1 Quilt around the motifs and in-the-ditch around the blocks. The frames can also be quilted in-the-ditch. Quilt the border with lines following the plaid design on your fabric.

2 Trim the layers evenly to allow for a 0.75 cm binding, then stitch a line of permanent basting around the edges within the seam allowance.

3 Attach the binding with a 0.75 cm seam. Fold to the back and blind-hem into place, to finish 0.75 cm wide.

4 Sign and date the quilt to finish.

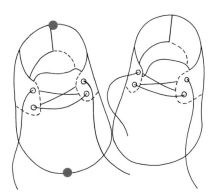

Enlarge templates to 10 cm between the red dots

Reverse Appliqué

· ·

As its name suggests, this technique is the reverse of the usual process of appliqué: instead of applying shapes to a background, shapes are cut out of the background fabric to reveal the design beneath. Enthusiasts of the method say that it is possible to work details with greater precision. It is important for the stability of the whole design to keep the grain lines of the background fabric and the motifs consistent.

MAKING A SAMPLE BLOCK

1 From the pattern on page 177, enlarge just the flower and the leaves from the corner to 15 x 15 cm. Choose three fabrics, one each for the flower, centre and leaves.

2 From calico, cut one 18 cm square for the background. Finger-press centre lines on the square and use these for positioning, right side up, over the pattern. Trace the design onto the background square.

3 With the grain of both fabrics matching, place the flower fabric

right side up behind the motif on the calico square. Cut a square 1.25 cm larger than the flower motif. Pin the layers together with the calico on top.

4 Working on the right side of the calico (flower fabric beneath), baste 0.75 cm around the drawn shape.

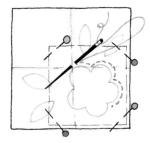

5 Carefully cut away the calico background fabric (which is on top) about 0.25 cm away from the drawn line within the flower shape to reveal the flower fabric below.

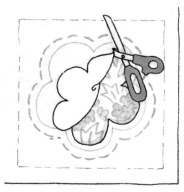

6 Matching the thread to the background, sew the background to the exposed flower fabric, using the needle-turning method *(see page 125)* and blind-hemming. Clip concave curves into the turning as necessary,

sewing with small stitches close together to stop fabric from fraying.

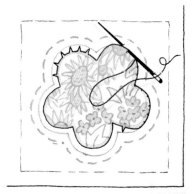

7 When the whole shape is stitched, remove the basting, turn the work over and trim away the excess flower fabric, leaving a 0.25 cm seam allowance all around.

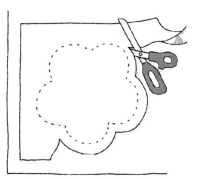

8 To make the leaves, cut a rectangle of leaf fabric for each leaf and follow steps 3–7 to appliqué.

9 Mark the flower fabric with the flower centre and baste a scrap of fabric beneath. Cut the centre of the flower fabric 0.25 cm away from the drawn line, then needle-turn and blind-hem the seam allowance under.

Butterflies Quilt

Skill level Beginner/Intermediate
Finished size 61 x 61 cm
Size of block 30.5 x 30.5 cm
Number of blocks 4

Materials

♦ 70 cm backing
♦ 70 cm wadding
♦ 70 cm white on calico
♦ 25 cm light green print for binding and stems
♦ Fat eighths of green prints x 2; multi-colour pastels x 2 for butterfly wings; bright floral x 1 for flowers
♦ Scraps of red, pink and beige prints for flower centres and fragmented wings
♦ Matching sewing and quilting thread
♦ Embroidery thread

Cutting

♦ Enlarge the block design on page 177 to 30.5 x 30.5 cm.

♦ For the fragmented wings, trace the wing and divide it into 12 straight-line sections for foundation piecing. Make two copies on tracing paper, one in reverse, adding a 1.25 cm seam allowance to both.

White on calico

♦ Cut four squares, each 33 cm. After working, trim to 32 cm.

♦ Cut the remainder of fabrics as needed.

Right: Butterfly with fragmented wings

Sewing

1 Place each block in turn over the pattern and trace the outlines of the shapes to be sewn. Mark each stem with a broken line.

2 Work the flowers and leaves as directed on page 139.

3 For the stems, cut a long rectangle to fit behind the length of the stem. Cut along the broken line and turn under a scant 0.25 cm on both sides to make narrow stems. Trim excess fabric.

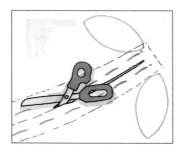

4 Work the four bodies and two sets of wings as directed on page 139.

5 For the butterflies with fragmented wings, use the sew-and-flip method *(see page 82)* and work two pairs of wings over the tracings made earlier. Piece from one end to the other.

6 Place a fragmented wing behind the wing drawn on the block. Cut and sew as before. Trim excess from back of the block. Repeat to add all remaining wings to complete the blocks.

7 Embroider the antennae. Press, face down. Trim blocks to 32 cm square. Arrange the blocks and join.

8 Mark the quilting design 0.75 cm away from the shapes, except for stems. On the background, mark a 5 cm diagonal grid. Mark the round corners. Layer and baste.

Finishing

1 Work the quilting from the centre outwards. Insert permanent basting around the edges and trim to 0.75 cm.

2 From the light green, make 2.8 m of 3 cm bias and bind to finish 0.75 cm wide. Sign and date your quilt.

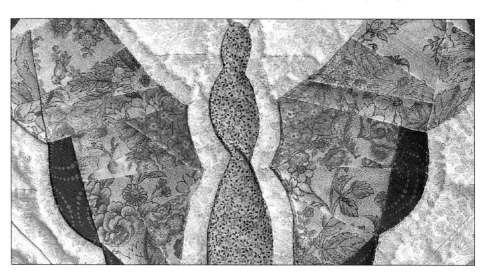

Hawaiian Appliqué

The Hawaiian quilt is characterised by its design, generally an eight-fold repeat reminiscent of the paper cut-outs many of us made as children. In the same way, Hawaiian quilters cut into the whole piece of folded cloth. This large single design is worked in one solid colour, such as red, blue or green, and appliquéd with a blind-hem stitch to a white background. The designs are often very intricate and take their inspiration from local flora. Figurative images are considered unlucky. Tradition has it that each quilt top (the kapa lau) must be a unique design – copying another's pattern is frowned upon by the Hawaiian quilting community.

MAKING A 30 CM BLOCK

1 Fold a 30 cm square of paper three times as illustrated below.

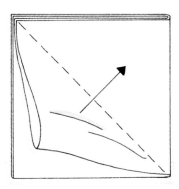

2 Draw a design with connecting parts on the folded edges. Shade in the parts to be cut out. Staple the parts to be cut away to prevent the paper from shifting while cutting *(see drawing at top of next column).*

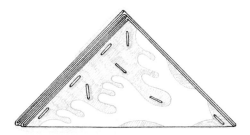

3 Cut out your design and unfold. Refold the design three times as before. The design can be revised by refolding the paper and making further cuts.

4 Make a template of the folded design (one-eighth of the whole).

5 Fold a 30 cm square of a single-colour fabric in the same way that you folded the paper. Press between each fold, then baste layers in place. Position the template, draw around it, and baste again within the design area.

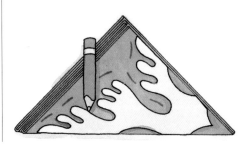

6 Cut out the shape, adding a 0.5 cm turning. The cut fabric should be handled as little as possible to avoid stretching its shaped edges.

7 Unfold and centre, right side up, over the right side of the 33.5 cm background square. Pin and baste the appliqué 1 cm away from the edges.

8 Begin sewing the marked section, working from the centre outwards. Clip into the seam allowance on concave curves as you come to them. Needle-turn the edge under along the drawn line, then blind-hem with thread that matches the top fabric.

9 Layer the block, then echo-quilt around the appliqué *(see page 156).*

Hawaiian Small Quilt

Skill level Intermediate/Advanced
Finished size 106.75 x 106.75 cm

Materials

♦ 2.3 m white (includes backing)
♦ 1.2 m wadding, 150 cm wide
♦ 1.4 m medium blue solid
♦ Matching sewing and quilting thread

Cutting

♦ Enlarge the design on page 179 and make a template of the design.

♦ To make the details, some parts of the design are marked as a slit on the template. The shape will become visible when seam allowances are turned under on both sides of the slit.

White
♦ Divide into two pieces, each 1.15 m long. Set one aside for the backing.

Medium blue
♦ Cut an 84 cm square for the appliqué, then use your template to cut out the shape on the drawn line.

♦ From the remainder, make 4.2 m bias binding, 4 cm wide, following the instructions on page 172. You will need a rectangle 23 x 97 cm, or equivalent.

Sewing

1 Make centre folds on both the white and the blue fabrics. Position the cut-out blue right side up over the white and baste the layers.

2 Sew the appliqué to the background, matching the thread to the blue top fabric and blind-hemming neatly in place. Secure the slits by turning each side under 0.5 cm and blind-hemming.

3 To make the scalloped border, follow the directions on page 169.

4 Assemble the quilt layers *(see page 31)* and baste together.

Finishing

1 Quilt in-the-ditch around the blue appliqué with blue thread. Add internal lines of blue about 1.25 cm inside its edges and small enclosed shapes within these where space permits. Quilt the enclosed background shapes with a line 1.25 cm inside the shape. Echo-quilt the rest of the background with lines 1.25 cm apart.

2 Insert permanent basting all around the edges of the quilt outside the marked scalloped line. Trim the excess fabrics and wadding to leave a 1 cm seam. Add the bias binding with a 1 cm seam, folding it to the back of the quilt and blind-hemming to a 1 cm finished width. Make a hanging sleeve *(see page 35)*. Sign and date to finish.

Mola Appliqué

A close relative of reverse appliqué, this method also involves working with several layers of fabric, building up the design from the bottom and cutting away parts of the top layer. The style is associated with the San Blas islands off the coast of Panama; a mola is a woman's blouse that has been decorated front and back with a reverse appliqué panel, traditionally worked in bright solid colours. The main effect is of shapes echoed by successive outlines of colour. Mola work includes conventional appliqué and inlay, a technique in which small slits are made in the top layer of fabric and contrasting colours are inserted. Besides wall hangings and pictures, the technique is ideal for cushions, vests and bags. Mola projects are usually not quilted, although a thin layer of flannel may be inserted between the front and the backing to add stability.

MAKING A SAMPLE BLOCK

1 Assemble solid black, blue, ochre and red 100 percent cotton fabric scraps, each approximately 28 x 18 cm; tracing paper; and sewing and embroidery thread. Always match thread to the fabric being applied.

2 Cut a rectangle of black fabric 28 x 18 cm for the background.

3 Place a layer of blue fabric right side up over the right side of the black. Pin or baste the layers together. Make a tracing of the large cat-body pattern *(see page 178)*. Baste the tracing over the blue and, with basting thread, work running stitches along the design lines as a guide to blind-hemming.

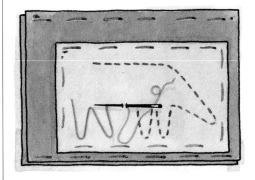

4 Carefully tear away the tracing, leaving the design marked in thread underneath.

5 Cut into the top layer (blue) about 0.25 cm away from the running-stitch line outside the cat shape.

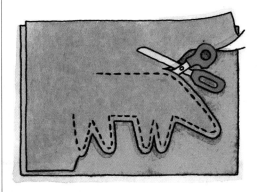

6 Needle-turn under and blind-hem, cutting the marker running stitches as you go. Keep your stitching close together. Clip into tight corners as necessary. Remove excess fabric *(see drawing at the top of next column).*

7 To add a third colour (ochre) outside the cat, cut a rectangle at least 2.5 cm larger than the hemmed shape. Baste in position, right side up.

8 The stitched cat outline will appear on the back of the work. Working 0.25 cm outside this outline, baste a line of running stitches through all layers; this marks where the new colour will be hemmed.

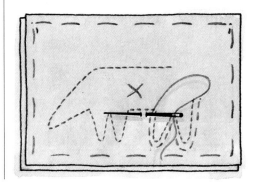

9 Turn back to the top of the work and cut 0.25 cm inside the line. Turn in the edge and blind-hem to the line, removing the stitches as you go. This leaves a black channel 0.25 cm wide between the two colours.

10 Place the fourth (red) rectangle over the panel, right side up. Pin or baste the layers.

Turn the work to the back. The cat should be visible as parallel lines of stitching in two different colours – blue inner line and ochre outer line. With basting thread and a running stitch, mark around the cat, inside and outside, 0.25 cm away from the respective lines of stitching. Be sure to

go through all layers so that it is visible on the top (red) when you turn the panel right side up. The running-stitch lines mark where you will blind-hem. Cut 0.25 cm away from the lines, inside or outside as appropriate, turn under, and blind-hem the raw edge.

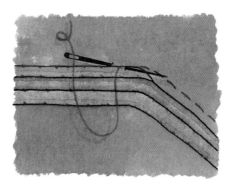

11 Using the conventional needle-turning method, appliqué the cat's head, first in blue, then in red, over the raw edges of the neck.

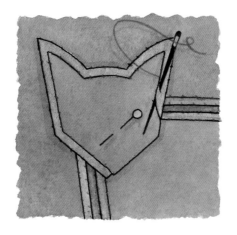

12 Decorate the area around the cat with triangles of inlay *(see detail below)*. Into the red make a small three-way cut and insert a scrap of another colour. Turn under the little points of the top layer and blind-hem.

13 Embroider such details as whiskers and eyes with a running stitch *(see detail below)*.

14 Back and bind the block to finish.

Below: Detail of *Mola Wall Hanging* project *(see page 146 for instructions).*

Mola Wall Hanging

Skill level Advanced
Finished size 81.5 x 66 cm

Materials

- 1.4 m black for backing
- 1 m garnet red
- 70 cm blue
- 70 cm ochre
- 50 cm pink
- 25 cm ochre and rust stripe
- 25 cm emerald-green
- 25 cm warm yellow
- 20 cm dark green
- Basting, sewing and embroidery thread

Cutting

- From the templates provided on pages 177–178, enlarge the design for the cats' heads, bodies and leaf twigs.

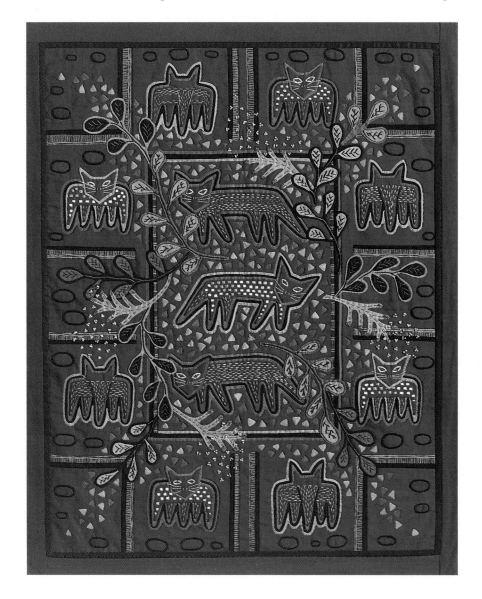

Black
- Cut a piece 84 x 69 cm for backing.

- Cut a rectangle 76.5 x 61.5 cm for the background.

- Cut two strips 2.5 x 76.5 cm and two strips 2.5 x 61.5 cm for the inner borders.

Garnet red
- Cut a rectangle 76.5 x 61.5 cm.

- Cut two strips 4.5 x 84 cm and two strips 4.5 x 63.5 cm for the outer border.

- Cut strips 3 cm wide to total 3.05 m for the binding.

Blue
- Cut a rectangle 76.5 x 61.5 cm.

- The remaining pieces are cut later.

Sewing

1 On the black background mark the design areas with basting; use the photograph as a guide.

2 For the centre panel, make tracings of the cat body: two facing left and one facing right. For the borders, make four tracings of the front-view body and four of the back-view body.

3 Place the second layer of fabric (blue) right side up over the right side of the black. Baste the layers together, including a line around the central area of the panel. One at a time, baste the tracings in place over the blue and, with basting thread, work running

stitches along the design lines. Mark the centre side-view cats, the lower back-view cat in the left-hand border and the top back-view cat in the right-hand border. Tear away the tracings.

4 Cut into the blue 0.25 cm away from the running-stitch line outside the first centre cat shape. Needle-turn under and blind-hem. Repeat for the two other centre cats.

5 Repeat the process to cut and turn in the blue around the central area towards the border side. There will be some blue fabric in the centre that can now be removed.

6 Repeat the process for the lower-left and top-right side cats.

7 The remaining border cats have yellow or pink bodies, so they need a slightly different treatment. Begin with the top left-hand side cat. Remove the blue rectangle from the appropriate basted area. Keep intact, as it will be used in step 11 to help vary the cats' colour scheme. Into the space, put an equivalent piece of warm yellow. Baste a front cat-body tracing on top. With running stitches and basting thread, mark the outline. Cut 0.25 cm away outside the running stitches, then blind-hem into place, again removing the running stitches as you go. In the same way, work the lower right-hand side cat.

8 Repeat step 7 to work the pink cats on the top and bottom borders. All the cats should now have body shapes against the black background.

9 Baste and appliqué strips of striped fabric on the inner side of the centre panel and on the small side panels. These will have some raw edges, which will be covered by the red layer.

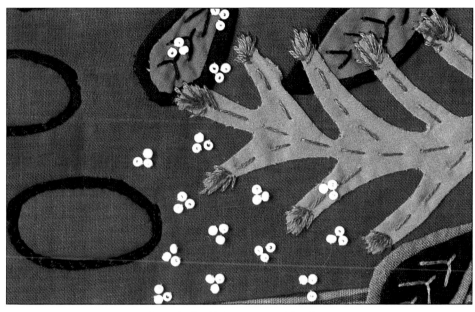

Detail of pebbles, twigs and beading

10 To add the ochre outside the centre cat, cut a rectangle at least 2.5 cm larger than the hemmed shape. Pin or baste in position right side up and proceed as in step 4 on page 144. Repeat to add pink around the top and bottom centre cats.

11 To add blue outside the first yellow cat, replace the rectangle removed earlier. Repeat step 10 to add blue outside the pink cats on the bottom left and top right. Add ochre outside the remaining top, bottom and side cats.

12 Place the red rectangle over the panel, right side up. Baste the layers and proceed as in step 5 on page 144. To complete the fourth layer, repeat marking and sewing around the separate panels.

13 Over the raw edges of the necks on the centre cats, appliqué the heads, first in blue, then red.

14 Cut and apply the leafy twigs. Add separate leaves and chain stitch the stems.

15 Decorate the background with pebble shapes and inlay triangles in bright colours *(see step 11 on page 145)*. To make a pebble *(see above)*, mark an oval and baste the centre. Cut along the marked line. Needle-turn the red fabric away from the line on both sides and blind-hem to secure.

16 Using the photograph as a guide, embroider the details and add the beads.

Finishing

1 Trim the panel to 60 x 74.5 cm. Attach the narrow black inner-border strips to all four sides. Add the red outer borders *(see page 168)*.

2 Place the backing right side down with the panel on top right side up. Baste all around the edges. Add the binding, turn it over to the back and blind-hem in place.

3 Make and attach a hanging sleeve *(see page 35)*. Sign and date the wall hanging.

Stained-glass Appliqué

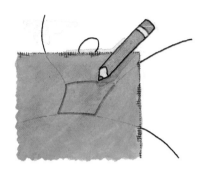

To create the appearance of stained glass in fabrics, narrow strips of black bias representing the lead are appliquéd around the coloured fabric shapes. Solid fabrics have the most impact. Hand-dyed fabrics or self-patterned commercial prints contribute visual interest by simulating the colour and texture variations found in old glass. Although black is the most common choice for the bias strips between the shapes, it is possible to choose other dark shades. The bias strips are usually applied by hand, although they can be blind-hemmed by machine.

MAKING A SAMPLE TURTLEDOVE BLOCK

1 Assemble a square of light-coloured background fabric and scraps of colours for the glass. You also need a 38 cm square of a fine black cotton fabric for the lead, along with basting and black sewing thread.

2 Enlarge one of the designs on page 180 to a diameter of 25.5 cm. Decide on the colour placement and label the appliqué shapes accordingly.

3 Take each colour in turn and, matching the grain line of the appliqué to that of the background, place right side up over the design and trace off the relevant shape. Where adjacent shapes are the same colour, cut as one piece but mark the lines between the parts. Also trace details

like veins on leaves when they exist in the design. Leave space between each piece for cutting with a scant 0.25 cm seam allowance. For dark fabrics, trace and cut out a paper template first to use for marking.

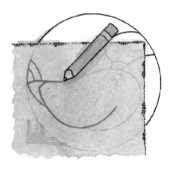

To mark detail lines, cut the template and trace along the required edge.

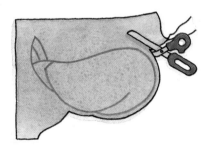

4 Tape the background fabric, right side up, over the design and trace with a fine pencil line.

5 Pin each appliqué piece over the design. The pencil outlines on the

shapes should exactly match with those on the ground. Where two fabrics meet, their seam allowances will overlap and all the pencil lines should coincide.

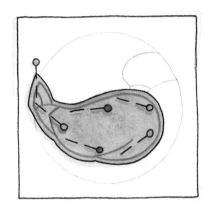

6 With running stitches, baste all the edges along the pencil lines through all the layers. These stitches remain in the work and will be covered by the bias later.

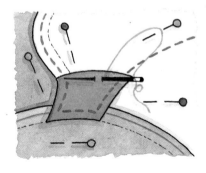

7 Do not use purchased bias tape for stained-glass appliqué. Prepare bias in the following manner:

(a) Using the 45° angle on your quilter's rule or a set square, cut a triangle shape from the corner of the black fabric. Lay the ruler overlapping the bias edge by 2 cm and cut off a strip. Repeat to cut several strips. Cut more strips as needed to complete the design.

(b) Prepare the strips by placing right side down as directed by Preparing Stems on page 124 and pressing. If your first attempt is wobbly, spray with a fine mist of water and try again. Avoid distorting the strip.

8 Work one strip at a time. Plan ahead to determine the sequence of strips to ensure neat ends and unnecessary overlapping of strips.

9 With the raw edge down, pin, then blind-hem around the appliqué shape.

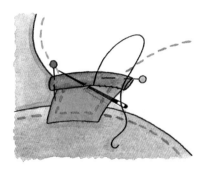

Where possible, sew inside curves first. If there is a sharp angle, fold the bias like a mitre, although the angle must suit the design. Add an extra stitch across this fold to secure it as invisibly as you can.

Sometimes a strip may be partly sewn with a gap left along one side to accommodate another strip that will be tucked in later (see below).

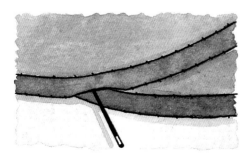

10 If an end will be covered by another strip, trim to 0.25 cm, then continue with the next strip in sequence until the design is complete.

11 If your machine has a blind-hem stitch, it can be used to attach the bias strips. Work as for the hand method; remember, though, that the bias strips need to be basted in place before machine blind-hemming.

Always work a test first to make sure the tension is not too tight and that the stitch will penetrate the bias without being conspicuous. A satin stitch or appliqué foot may feed the work through the machine more evenly.

12 Make a French knot for the eye with stranded embroidery thread (see illustration on page 132).

PROJECT
Window Hanging

Window Hanging

Skill level Intermediate
Finished size 106.5 x 91.5 cm
Block size 40.75 x 40.75 cm
Number of blocks 4

Materials

♦ 1 m sheer iridescent fabric
♦ 1.9 m black – 100 percent cotton
♦ 1.4 m charcoal or black print
♦ 40 cm white on white
♦ 25 cm each sky-blue, golden yellow, scarlet, apple-green, emerald-green, bright purple
♦ Scraps of light grey, medium grey and rust
♦ Sewing thread
♦ 1 brass hanging ring
♦ Two 89 cm lengths of thin dowel
♦ 1 m medium-weight iron-on interfacing

Cutting

♦ Enlarge the designs of the birds in the roundels to 25.5 cm in diameter. On paper, draw a 40.75 cm square containing a 5 cm-wide frame and divide into irregular shapes.

♦ From patterns on pages 179–180, make templates for the tab and the pediment, and label.

Charcoal or black print
♦ Cut one lower border 94 x 11.5 cm, two top borders 94 x 6.5 cm, and two side-border strips 84 x 11.5 cm.

♦ Place the edge marked 'fold' on the pediment template on the folded edge of the fabric and cut two pediments.

♦ To estimate the width of the rod pockets, measure the diameter of the dowel, add 4 cm, then double. Cut strips 93 cm long by this width.

♦ From scraps, cut a tab for the hanging ring.

♦ Cut two strips 84 x 2.75 cm and four strips 43.5 cm x 2.75 cm for setting the blocks.

Interfacing
♦ Cut two strips 91.5 x 5 cm and two strips 81.5 x 5 cm.

♦ Cut one pediment without seam allowances.

Sheer iridescent fabric
♦ Cut four squares, each 46 cm.

♦ The remaining fabrics are cut when working the appliqué.

Sewing

1 Lightly finger-press a vertical and horizontal crease in the iridescent blocks. Use them to centre the blocks over the bird designs, then trace the design onto the fabric in pencil. Take care not to graze the fabric.

2 Working as directed on page 148, cut and baste fabrics for all the required shapes.

3 Prepare bias strips and sew to the design. Work the bird first, then add the five strips that support the roundel in the square, then the roundel. Make the join in the strip around the

roundel to coincide with one of the lower supporting strips. Add the strips to cover all the raw edges in the frame. Add the bias to the inner square.

4 Turn the block over and sew the bias strips to the back following the same sequence.

5 Complete all blocks on both sides and trim to 42.25 cm square. The side on which the coloured fabrics have been placed is the front. Arrange the blocks in two rows of two blocks.

Assembly

1 Use a 0.75 cm seam allowance throughout for the assembly. To join the blocks so the hanging is reversible, place one short setting strip right side up on the front of the block and another right side up with the reverse of the same edge – the block is

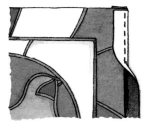

sandwiched between the two setting strips. Sew. Press setting strips away from the block, enclosing the block edge. On the other long edge of the front short setting strip, place the next block, front side down, and sew.

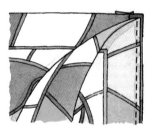

Press the seam allowance within the setting strip. Now fold the reverse setting strip into place, turning under the raw edge level with the front setting strip, and blind-hem into place.

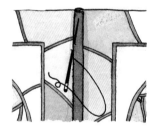

Repeat to join the two lower blocks. Then repeat, using the longer setting strips to join the top and bottom rows of blocks.

2 Attach the iron-on interfacing to the pediment and to border strips.

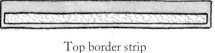

Top border strip

Lower border strip

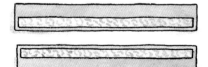

Side border strips

3 Sew the shorter border strips to the sides of the centre panel. Fold them in half, turn in 0.75 cm, and blind-hem the edge to the reverse against the blocks. Add one long strip to the bottom edge in the same way.

4 Place two pediment pieces right sides together and sew except for the long lower edge. Turn right side out and press. Place the two top-border strips right sides together and sew across both short ends. Do not turn out. Sandwich the pediment between the top-border strips, right sides together, and sew the long seam. Turn the border strips right side out. Place right sides together on the front of the panel and sew the long seam. Fold the pediment unit over to the back of the hanging to enclose.

5 Fold the tab in half, right sides together, then sew. Turn right side out and press. Fold in half the other way around the brass hanging ring and place to the reverse of the pediment at the top. Sew securely in place by hand.

6 To make up the two rod pockets, follow the directions for making a hanging sleeve on page 35, making a 0.75 cm hem across the short ends and a much narrower tube. Place at the top and bottom of the hanging on the reverse and sew by hand. Slide the dowels inside and lightly stitch the ends to secure the rods.

7 Sign and date the hanging to finish *(see page 167)*.

Below: Detail of Swan roundel

Shadow Appliqué

....

In this method, the appliqué design is trapped between an opaque background fabric and a translucent or sheer top layer, such as voile, georgette, chiffon, organza or iridescent sheer. The assembled layers are held in place with small running stitches around the outline of the appliqué design. The secret of a good design lies in the choice of fabric used for the motifs in the middle layer.

MAKING A POPPY BLOCK

1 Enlarge the poppy design *(see page 186)* to fit a 15 cm block. Cut a 15 cm square for the background and trace the design onto it. For the top layer, cut a 15 cm sheer fabric square.

2 Trace the poppy onto red cotton. Cut out without seam allowances. From black cotton, cut the flower centres without a seam allowance. Handle the shapes as little as possible.

3 Baste the red poppy, then the black centre, on the background without knotting the thread. (Adjacent shapes, if any, should lie edge to edge.)

4 Place the sheer fabric right side up on top. Pin and baste.

5 Using thread that matches the appliqué shape, sew around the outer edge of the flower centre with a small running stitch. To make sure the shape does not shift, add a second line 0.25 cm inside the raw edge of the shape. Repeat with each shape. Use thread to match the background for the line of running stitches around the petals, and red thread for the stitching within the shape.

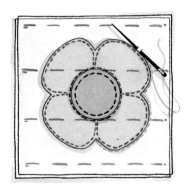

6 Using the template on page 186 as a guide, stem stitch the stamens.

7 Remove the basting stitches and lightly press.

PROJECT

*Shadow Appliqué
Wall Hanging*

Skill level Beginner
Finished size 56 x 56 cm

Materials

- 70 cm white for backing
- 70 cm wadding
- 50 cm sheer white for the top
- 50 cm bright purple
- 25 cm lilac
- 25 cm holly green
- Scraps of bright red, deep red, pink, blue-violet and bright green
- Bright green wool for stems

Cutting

- Use the photograph as a guide *(see pages 185–187 for patterns)*. For the tulip stem, draw a 34 cm line on your background fabric. Make templates for any shapes too dark to be traced off the design.

White
- Cut a 43.5 cm background square.

- Cut a 61 cm square for the backing.

Bright purple
- Cut strips 4 cm wide and totalling 2.4 m for the binding.

- Cut four strips, each 58.5 x 6 cm, for the outer border.

- Cut one tulip and 20 grapes.

Lilac
- Cut four strips, each 51 x 4 cm, for the middle border.

Green
♦ Cut four strips, each 46 x 4.5 cm, for the inner border.

Coloured scraps
♦ From bright red, cut two poppies, one inner tulip shape and 10 small petals for the lower flowers.

♦ Cut two dark red flower centres.

♦ Cut two pink petals for tulips.

♦ Cut one vase in blue-violet.

♦ Cut two large flowers and two leaves in bright green.

Sewing

1 Place the white background fabric over the design. Where the design shows through, position all the shapes, pinning and basting each in turn. Lightly mark the stems in pencil as a single broken line.

2 Place the sheer fabric on top and baste thoroughly.

3 Use a running stitch to sew around and inside the shapes.

4 To make the stems using trapunto quilting, sew one line of small running stitches at each side of the broken lines *(fig. 1)*. Double a length of thread, then thread the loop through the eye of a large needle. The doubled thread must be longer than the stem to be filled. Insert the needle from the back of the work through the backing only into one end of the channel between the two lines of stitching *(fig. 2)*. Thread the needle up the channel between the backing and the layers of sheer fabric. Make sure the loop of the sewing cotton remains outside on the surface. Remove the needle, leaving the thread in the channel. Thread a length of green wool through the sewing cotton loop and double it over *(fig. 3)*. Pull the sewing cotton, easing the green wool in between the fabric layers and out the other end. Snip both ends of the yarn *(fig. 4)*.

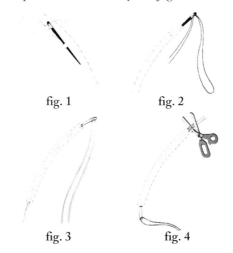

fig. 1   fig. 2

fig. 3   fig. 4

5 Remove the basting and press from the back. Trim to measure 41 x 41 cm. Assemble the inner-, middle- and outer-border strips into four sets. Attach to the four sides of the panel, mitring each corner *(see page 168)*. Layer the top *(see page 31)* and baste.

Finishing

1 Quilt in-the-ditch around the border strips.

2 Insert a row of permanent basting around the edges. Attach the binding strips with 1 cm seam. Fold to the back and blind-hem to 1 cm finish.

3 Make a hanging sleeve *(see page 35)*. Sign and date to finish.

QUILTING

The continuous running stitch that holds the layers of fabric and filling together is known as quilting. Depending on the design of the quilt and the quilter's skill, the quilting plan can be plain and unobtrusive, simply following the seams of the piecing, or it can be very elaborate, filled with intricate patterns of wreaths, feathers and flowers. Simple pieced designs of solid-colour fabrics, or whole cloth quilts, encourage intricate showcase quilting. These very elaborate quilting designs are favoured by the Amish, Welsh and northern English communities, each producing designs of outstanding beauty.

The warmth and texture of quilted cloth have appealed to people since antiquity, and the earliest known example that is recognisable as a quilt was found in a tomb near the Mongolian-Siberian border. Believed to date from between 100 B.C. and A.D. 200, it shows couched embroidery, spirals and diamond cross-hatching. In the early Middle Ages, soldiers wore tunics with stitched and filled parallel channels; knights wore quilted vests under their chain mail. In the seventeenth and eighteenth centuries, women wore quilted petticoats, bodices and waistcoats.

Much of the romance associated with quilt making comes from our knowledge of the quilting bee. This gathering of friends, family and neighbours functioned on two levels: first, as an expedient way of quilting tops that had been pieced during winter months (the dextrous fingers of five or six women around a frame could finish a quilt very quickly), and second, as a social occasion that offered a break from the chores of everyday life.

Left: Detail of a nineteenth-century *Bear's Paw* quilt

Preparation for Quilting

....

Whether you intend to hand or machine quilt or to use a combination of both, good preparation is vital. Decisions must be made about the quilting design and how it will be marked. The quilt layers must be assembled and secured.

CHOOSING THE DESIGN

Quilting may simply follow the design of a pieced or appliqué top – outline, in-the-ditch and echo-quilting. All three are popular because none need additional marking.

In-the-ditch refers to sewing along the seam lines or, in the case of appliqué, right next to the applied shapes. It is particularly good for beginners, as the actual stitches cannot be seen – only their effect.

In-the-ditch quilting

Outline quilting is stitched 0.75 cm away from the seam, appliqué design or printed motif on the fabric.

Echo-quilting is an echoing series of quilting lines stitched around the patchwork or appliqué shapes. Echo-

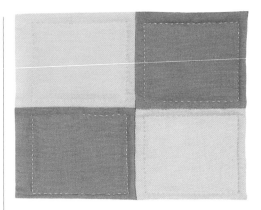

Outline quilting

quilting is stitched 0.75 cm away from the shape with all further quilting lines equally spaced. The effect is to throw the enclosed design into higher relief. It is an easy method for beginners who are ready to show off their improving stitches.

Other quilting patterns fall into three main groups: motifs, such as wreaths and flowers, often used centred in blocks or panels; running patterns, such as cables and running feathers, which contribute movement to a design and are often used in borders; and filling patterns.

Fillings are simple patterns often based on grids and used to fill in background areas. They provide an overall texture without distracting from the main design.

Filling quilting patterns

USING QUILTING TEMPLATES AND STENCILS

A template is a shape that is a guide for drawing; it suits simple motifs. If a shape is to be traced around many times, it should be made of durable material, such as template plastic.

Templates can include very simple forms that tessellate to make overall patterns and grids or that build into running patterns, such as a teardrop used to draft feather designs.

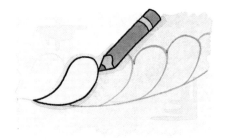

To mark the quilting pattern, place the template on a paper draft of the quilt, if at the designing stage, or directly on the quilt top, and draw around it. Move to the next position and repeat. With tessellating designs, place the template against one of the lines already marked and draw around the remaining shape. Such designs often need one or more baselines – these should not be drawn; instead, finger-press a line or add a strip of masking tape.

A stencil is a sheet of plastic with channels cut into it, along which you run your marking tool. It suits running designs like cables.

On commercial stencils, the

channels are interrupted by bars that help keep the design whole. They are also marked with centre lines and balance marks.

When using templates and stencils, keep track of which way the design is going. For example, when a design turns a corner, it often becomes a mirror image of itself. This indicates that the template or stencil needs to be flipped over.

MARKING

Before marking any of the design, test it against the intended space, marking repeats with pins. This avoids having to make a large adjustment to one single repeat. Decide how best to fit the design. It can be stretched, enlarged or compressed. You may think it is better to have one less repeat and to enlarge the last two or three repeats or else have an extra repeat and make them smaller.

Mark your quilt as little as possible and use the simplest marking methods, such as an H grade graphite pencil or the equivalent on light or medium fabrics. For dark fabrics, try a sliver of dry soap or a light or silver pencil. Whichever marker you choose, keep it well sharpened to maintain a fine, accurate line.

For marking filling patterns, masking tape is useful and helps you avoid having to draw many lines on your quilt. Only tape as much as you expect to sew in one sitting. Never leave tape on the quilt for any length of time or in bright sunlight. Simply place a length of tape on the proposed quilting line and quilt alongside. For a grid, quilt along both sides of the tape.

Self-adhesive plastic is suitable for making templates to your own specifications. Such templates can be used and repositioned several times before they no longer adhere. The same warning as for masking tape applies here.

An alternative is to draw the design on tracing paper and baste it to the quilt. Quilt the design through the paper, by hand or by machine, then tear the paper away. This works better for machine sewing than for handwork, as it allows you to add a design on an already layered quilt top.

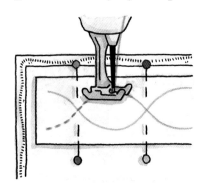

FUDGING

This term refers to modifying a design in subtle ways to make it fit an available space. In an ideal world, the quilting design is drafted to fit the project; however, you may be working with purchased templates whose size does not fit exactly into the space.

Because fudging means redrawing parts of the design, it is best to use the template for drawing the most complex parts. This helps fool the eye into thinking things are perfect! Then, to make the necessary changes, draw the simplest parts freehand to fit the space. Draw part of the template, then slip it to one side to continue drawing and to connect the parts freehand.

USING HOOPS AND FRAMES

After the quilt has been marked and layered, it is ready for quilting. Some experienced quilters are happy to quilt without the assistance of a frame. However, beginners will find a frame or hoop invaluable. A hoop stabilises the quilt layers, helping to create even tension and achieve a more consistent surface appearance.

A hoop consists of two wooden round or oval rings with a screw adjuster on the outer ring. Bind wooden hoops with cotton tape to avoid wood stains and to give good grip on the fabric. The hoop is moved from place to place over the quilt and keeps the work easily portable. Avoid overtightening; this can distort the quilt. Never leave the quilt fixed in the hoop when not quilting, as doing so can mark or distort the fabrics.

Smaller embroidery hoops or rings are useful for free-motion machine quilting. Some sewing machines will not form good stitches unless the layers are tensioned in an embroidery ring. The ring is moved from one part to another as work progresses.

A free-standing wooden frame in which the quilt layers are fixed for the entire quilting process provides the most even surface and allows several quilters to work at the same time.

Hand Quilting

The quilting stitch is a simple one. The challenge is to work it with small, evenly-sized stitches and spaces with the same appearance on both sides.

Beginners should aim for straight, even stitches. With practice, the size of the stitch can be reduced. It is useful to know that the size of any stitching will be affected by the weight of fabric and the texture of wadding, no matter how experienced the quilter. So expect some variation on different projects.

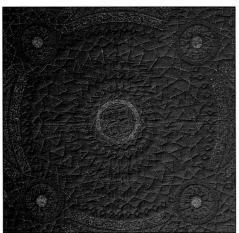

Above: Quilting seen from the front and back

QUILTING

1 Cut a 40–50 cm length of quilting thread. If it is not a pre-waxed thread, draw it across a piece of wax. Waxing helps the thread to glide through the quilt layers.

2 Thread the needle and make a small knot at one end. To make the knot, wind the thread around your forefinger and then pass the needle alongside the fingernail through the loop as illustrated. Pull the knot firmly into position at the end of the thread.

3 Start quilting from the centre and work outwards.

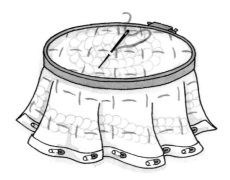

4 To hide the knot in the wadding, insert the point of the needle into the quilt top a short distance away from where you wish to start sewing and run the needle into the wadding

without going through to the backing. Bring the needle out where you wish to start and pull the thread until the knot stops on the quilt top. Give it a slight tug to 'pop' the knot through the top to the inside of the quilt.

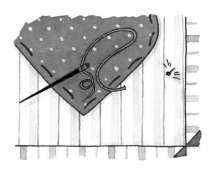

5 Work running stitches through all layers. To get them even, insert the needle vertically through all layers, then direct it forwards and up to the top of the work. This also helps reduce the amount of drifting that can occur between the three layers when one layer is pushed more than the others.

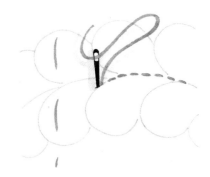

6 To keep the reverse of the quilt looking neat, the ends of thread must be finished off. Make a small backstitch, splitting the previous stitch to anchor it. Then insert the needle

Twentieth-century whole cloth quilt featuring an interlaced cable and running feather, medallion and cross-hatching quilting patterns.

through the layers without going through to the back and come out a short distance away, if possible along where the line of stitching will continue, because this will help secure it. Keep a very slight tension on the thread as you carefully cut it close to the surface and the end will slip back inside the layers.

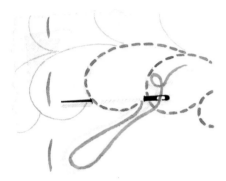

A quick and undetectable alternative is to make a knot in the thread and hide it in the wadding. The instructions are lengthy, but in fact it is easy to do.

MAKING KNOTS TO TIE OFF QUILTING

1 To get the knot in the correct position on the thread, lay the thread on the quilt in the direction in which your final stitch will be. Keep it in place with your left thumb (if right-handed).

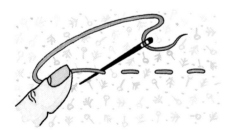

2 Slip the needle under the thread and rotate the needle over the thread and back under it. Put the point of the needle into the fabric in the right place to complete the last

stitch, passing the needle into the wadding only.

3 With the left thumb keeping the coil close to the quilt's surface, bring the needle out to the top of the work and pull through carefully. The knot should form tightly around the thread at just the correct point. As it reaches the fabric, a tiny tug will pop it into the wadding with the last stitch perfectly in place. Hold the thread firmly as you snip to encourage the tail to slip inside the wadding.

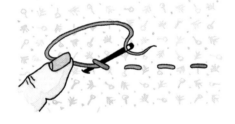

STAB-STITCH QUILTING

An alternative way to quilt is to use a stab-stitch rather than a true running stitch. Although the appearance is the same, stab-stitching requires two steps to make a single stitch and for this reason is thought to be slower.

To stab-stitch, position your preferred hand beneath the quilt because it will be the easier to control when you cannot see it. Holding the needle in your other hand, insert it through the quilt layers, catch it with the hand below, and push it back to the top of the work.

ROCKING THE NEEDLE

Many quilters find they need a second thimble on the finger beneath the work that directs the needle forwards. Use the fingers below to push against the layers, slightly compressing the wadding as the needle is pushed in and down. This makes it easier to get the needle back through to the top. Co-ordinating this action produces the rocking action described by many experienced quilters. With practice, the needle can be rocked to pick up a series of stitches on the needle before the thread is drawn through them all at one time.

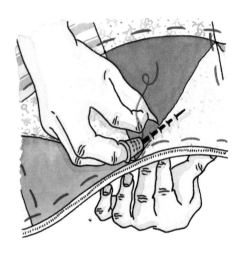

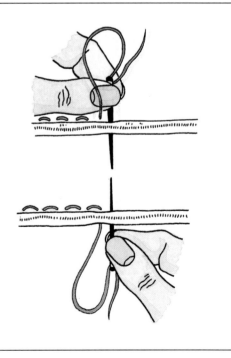

Trapunto

Above: Trapunto detail

The idea of sewing an enclosed shape on two layers of fabric, then stuffing it with some kind of filling, goes back a long way. Some of the earliest surviving quilts feature this technique. Trapunto combines well with other quilting styles when the surrounding is quilted, such as with a regular filling pattern or a meandering or stippled texture. Take care not to overstuff the shapes or the work will warp. Also, overstuffed shapes are the first to display signs of wear during use, their taut covering becoming quite threadbare while the rest of the quilt may still be in good condition.

MAKING A TRAPUNTO SAMPLE DESIGN

1 From calico, cut a square for the block top and mark with a design.

2 Cut a matching square of loosely-woven fabric, such as cheesecloth or turban muslin. Place behind the calico and baste together.

3 On the right side, by hand or by machine, quilt the drawn outlines.

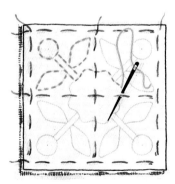

4 Turn to the back of the work to fill the shapes. If the backing is sufficiently loosely woven, you will be

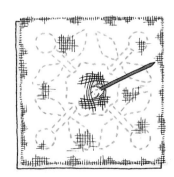

able to ease the threads open with a blunt knitting needle. Through the hole, insert tiny scraps of filling, such as wadding or trapunto wool. When filled, tease the threads back into place.

5 If the backing is too firmly woven, cut a small opening in the shape and fill. Sew the opening closed as neatly as possible without reducing the area of the background excessively.

Machine Quilting

·······································

Machine quilting necessitates preparation different from that of hand quilting but requires the same amount of practice to do well. Although it is possible to quilt with an all-purpose presser foot, a walking or an even feed foot encourages the three layers of the sandwich to pass through the machine at the same rate.

For free-motion quilting, see your sewing-machine manual for guidance on setting up to do this type of work. A darning foot will safeguard your fingers. Otherwise, remove the foot and be especially watchful of your fingers! Also drop the feed dogs, which carry the fabric through the machine from front to back, or cover them with a special throat plate. Some machines do not form good free-motion stitching unless the work is tensioned in an embroidery hoop – this can be discovered only by testing.

PREPARATION FOR MACHINE QUILTING

1 Use a size 80 needle and a regular mercerized-cotton sewing thread. Make a sandwich of calico and wadding to test your machine settings. Low-loft cotton wadding is recommended because cotton fabrics cling to it, reducing the amount of basting required and limiting the amount of movement that takes place.

2 Use safety pins for basting the layers. They can be removed or repositioned quickly during stitching. If thread-basting, put the basting to

one side of where you plan to quilt. Basting threads pierced by the quilting stitches are difficult to remove.

3 Sew a few centimetres on the sample to check the stitch length – usually 0.25 cm. Fabric can tear away from stitches that are too small, and large stitches do not have enough stretch to tolerate stress on the quilt during use.

4 When the stitch length is right, examine the tension. Because the quilt sandwich is thicker than a normal two-fabric layer, you may need to reduce the tension a little; however, the two threads should still lock together in the middle. This may be easier to see if you load different colours on top and in the bobbin.

5 Check whether your machine has a control to alter the amount of downward pressure on the presser foot. Machines are set for sewing two layers of fabric. As the quilt sandwich is thicker, it fills the space under the presser foot more, and slightly less pressure is needed. This reduces the tendency of the machine to push the layers through at different rates, which can cause the quilt to pucker.

6 Continuous lines make the quilting go more quickly and eliminates having to finish many thread ends. Practise tracing over designs to see how they can be modified for continuous stitching.

7 When beginning to sew, turn the balance wheel to insert the needle at the right place and draw the bobbin thread to the top. Hold both threads as you begin to sew to avoid the lower one becoming tangled underneath.

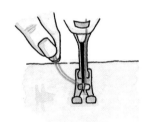

8 As you guide the work through the machine, hold it on each side of the needle with your fingertips and exert slight sideways pressure. On pieced tops, this opens up the ditch a little, helping the stitches to sink into the seam. Such tension also helps with free-motion work, reducing the need to fit the work into an embroidery hoop.

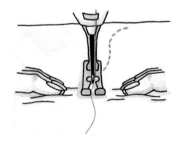

9 To reduce the effort of trimming the threads at the beginning and end of a line of stitching, set the machine stitch length to almost 0. Run the machine for a stitch or two, then increase the length to normal, preferably while slowly running the machine. Sew the line to about 2–2.5 cm from the end, then reduce the stitch length again to almost 0. Cut the threads, leaving tails of 6.5–8 cm. Thread both tails through a needle with a large eye. Insert the needle into the wadding only at the stitching and bring it out again a short distance away *(see fig. 1)*. Tension these slightly as you snip them so that they will pop back inside and be hidden *(see fig. 2)*.

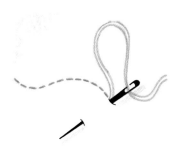

fig. 1

fig. 2

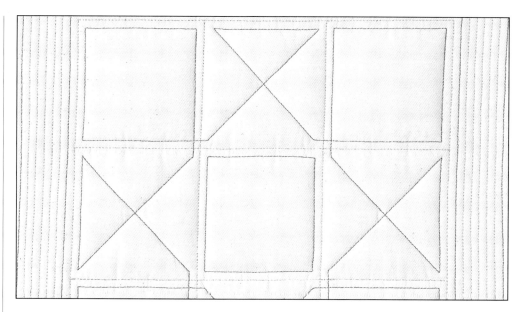

Above: Detail of machine quilting   Below: Free-motion machine quilting

Quilt-as-you-go

This term describes the technique of piecing and quilting at the same time by sewing the piecing shapes over the backing and wadding, which have been basted. By sewing through all layers, a quilted effect is achieved at the same time that the design is assembled. Some elements may need piecing before being added to the quilt. Add extra lines of quilting later, if necessary, to create symmetry of quilted patterns.

Making a Sample Block

1 Iron the backing, which should be 10–15 cm larger than the desired finished size. Place right side down on a flat surface.

2 Centre wadding of the same size on top. Pin and baste without knotting the ends of the basting threads. With a different colour thread, mark accurate centre lines vertically and horizontally. These ensure that the pieced design is positioned correctly on top.

3 Read the instructions for Machine Quilting on page 162 and set your machine accordingly.

4 Work out the sewing sequence. Starting from the centre, pin, baste, then sew each piece in turn until the design is complete.

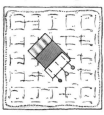 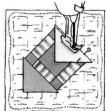

Sashiko Quilting

The Japanese word *sashiko refers to both the stitching and the grid-like patterns identified with the technique. It is worked over two layers of indigo-dyed cloth without wadding and was originally used to strengthen workmen's jackets. The stitches, worked in a heavy white thread, are about twice the size of the spaces between them.*

You can buy sashiko thread from quilting suppliers, or you can use coton à broder, cotton pearl, silk buttonhole twist and some grades of crochet cotton. Because very long threads are used, and the thread is pulled through the fabric many times, a twisted thread is needed. Stranded threads shred after a little while. The size of needle you use will be partly determined by the thread you select. It is traditional to pick up a series of stitches onto the needle before drawing it through the cloth. This makes the stitching quicker to work but requires a long needle. Any type of design can be worked in sashiko-style quilting.

MAKING A SAMPLE BLOCK

1 Enlarge your design, either on a photocopier, taping together several sheets to make an area of the correct size, or by drawing it up on graph paper to the measurements given with each pattern.

2 Mark the design on the right side of a 30 cm square of top fabric. Place over a second layer, wrong sides together, and baste.

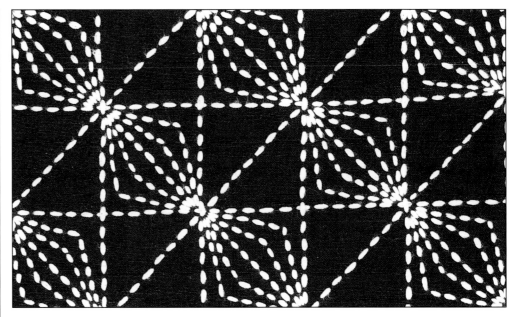

Above: Detail of Sashiko quilting

3 Using a running stitch, work the design in a logical way, either from the centre out or from one end of the block to the other. A grid is usually worked by sewing one line of the pattern across the whole area to be quilted. Then the second line is worked and so on until the design is complete.

4 Stitch size is often subtly adapted to fit the pattern being worked. However, good sashiko shows the same number of stitches on the same part of the design throughout. It is also necessary to adjust stitch size to turn corners because a corner can only be formed by the needle's entering or leaving the fabric. When multiple lines of a pattern meet, the preferred effect is to have a space at the centre on all lines, with stitches radiating from it like the petals of a flower.

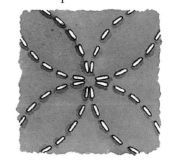

Tying and Seeding

....

Tying is a traditional way to secure the layers of a quilt together, particularly one with a thick filling. Often called comforters, these quilts were tied at quite large intervals, such as the corners or centres of blocks.

The thread can add an accent of colour when the tails are left long. Alternatively, the ties can be made inconspicuous and tied to the back and finished with a button.

Ties can be worked with narrow ribbon or with decorative embroidery thread and some knitting yarn. The only test is whether the yarn will travel through the quilt layers. If you want to include something too textured to pull through the layers easily, insert the textured yarn under the first stitch and then tie all ends together.

Ties with extra strands added to them for more volume are called tufts.

MAKING TIES AND TUFTS

1 Use a darning needle and a length of pearl cotton or crochet cotton. Ties can be worked with a double strand of thread or more. If threading several strands through, these can be a mixture of colours.

2 Make a stitch through all layers where the tie will be (fig. 1). Then make a second stitch at the same place and use a square knot to fasten the ends (figs. 2 and 3).

After working all the ties, trim the ends to the desired length.

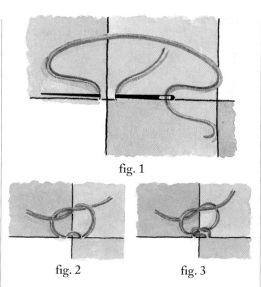

fig. 1

fig. 2   fig. 3

3 For speed and convenience, ties may be worked consecutively. Put a long length of doubled thread in the needle. Start where the first tie will be with the basic two stitches. With the thread still attached, move to the next place and make two stitches. Continue in the same way until the thread is used. Make sure there is enough length left between ties for tying the knots (see drawing below).

Take care not to draw up the quilt as the thread is carried from one tie to the next. Snip the thread between the stitches and tie the ends in the usual way with a square knot.

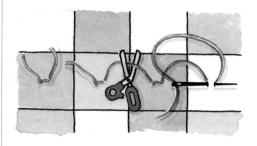

Making continuous ties

Detail of a quilt with wool-yarn tufting

SEEDING

Seeding is related to tying, although it might be considered more an embroidery stitch than a quilting one. It combines well with tying, anchoring the layers at regular intervals like ties but with a less noticeable appearance.

To make a seed stitch, work two small stitches next to each other, then pass the needle through the wadding, bringing it out where you will place the next seed. The maximum distance between seeds is determined by the length of the needle.

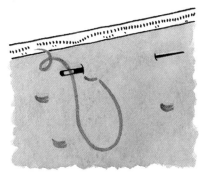

FINISHING

After all the hours you spend on making a quilt, it is worth finishing it with the same attention to detail as when you first embarked on the project. Do not skimp on or rush this step, which, when well executed, will contribute to the life of the quilt. If your quilt design needs a fancy finish, you might consider prairie points or scallops.

Finishing is the final framing device and your last chance to add an accent of colour. A narrow strip of colour can inject a surprising amount of sparkle or resonance into a quilt design.

Always sign and date your work. Most quilters enjoy naming their quilts, so include the title if you have one. If the title is inspired by a quotation, a piece of poetry or an event, make a note of this, too. If the quilt is a gift, say whom it is for and whether it has been made for a special purpose.

Labels can be written with a variety of markers specially produced for writing on fabric. Written labels allow you to include the most information. They can also be sewn using either hand or machine embroidery. Cross-stitch labels can be worked using a scrap of canvas waste basted to the label fabric. Labels can be decorated with stenciled, printed or stamped designs as long as the dye or ink is permanent. A label can be made from an extra pieced block or decorated with appliqué motifs as used on the front. If you wish to keep related materials, such as documents, with the quilt, make the label as a pocket or fabric envelope sewn to the back of the quilt.

When your quilt is finished, protect it from light, dust and damp. Ideally, it is best stored flat on a spare bed, covered with a sheet. Whichever storage method you choose, air your quilt from time to time, and never wrap it in plastic.

Left: Twentieth-century *Medallion*-style quilt

Borders

. . . .

The border is the frame that holds your quilt design together and helps unify all the components. The colour, type and size should be considered carefully. An imposing border might overshadow the quilt centre while a well-chosen border can bring a weak centre to life. With a bed quilt, the border is the part most handled, so it must be well constructed and thoroughly quilted.

Measure across the centre of the quilt, vertically and horizontally, to find the required border lengths. Cut borders for your project a little oversize as insurance.

BUTTED BORDERS

1 Determine your border width. Cut two strips the width x the length of the quilt side. Cut two strips the border width x the length of the quilt width, plus twice the border width. For example, for a 91.5 x 127 cm quilt with 15.5 cm borders, cut two side borders, each 15.5 x 127 cm; for the top and bottom borders, cut strips 15.5 x 122.5 cm.

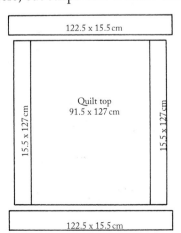

122.5 x 15.5 cm

15.5 x 127 cm

Quilt top
91.5 x 127 cm

15.5 x 127 cm

122.5 x 15.5 cm

2 Divide the quilt side and the side borders into halves and quarters. With right sides facing and raw edges level, match these points and pin across the seam line. Continue pinning, easing the top onto the border, then sew carefully.

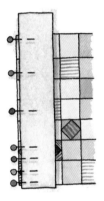

3 Check the appearance before pressing. Trim any excess, ensuring that the corner of the quilt is square. Repeat to add the opposite border.

4 Add top and bottom borders and check before pressing. The borders should lie flat when the quilt lies on a flat surface. Trim any excess *(see drawing at the top of next column).*

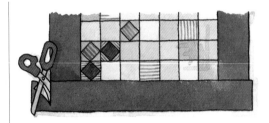

MITRED BORDERS

Making the required 45° angle at the corner for the mitre uses more fabric and requires careful handling of the bias seams.

1 Decide on the border width. Double this figure and add to both measurements for cutting the borders. To add a 15.5cm border to a 91.5 x 127 cm quilt top, cut two strips 127 x 15.5 cm and two 122.5 x 15.5 cm.

2 As in step 2 for butted borders, divide the quilt and border edges and pin borders to opposite sides of the quilt top.

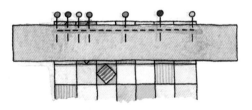

3 Start sewing the first border 0.75 cm from the corner, using a 0.75 cm seam allowance, and stop 0.75 cm from the end. Fold borders already attached out of the way and repeat to add the remaining borders.

4 To find where to sew the mitre seam, with the quilt wrong side up, fold both border ends at each corner as follows:

(a) Finger-press a continuation of the 0.75 cm seam that attaches the border and pin temporarily.

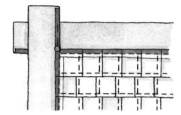

(b) Fold the end back along the border so the pinned turning is level with the existing seam. This makes a fold at right angles to the first seam, in line with the other seam coming to the corner. Lightly finger-press this fold.

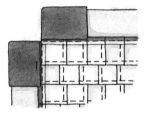

(c) Grasp the end of the border and bring it out to the side of the quilt to align the pinned turning with the fold just made in step b. This makes a 45° angled fold at the end of the border. Finger-press without stretching. Repeat for the other border strip.

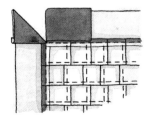

5 Fold the quilt top right sides together diagonally through the corner so that the two mitre folds are on top of each other. Pin across the fold. Before sewing, check that they lie together neatly without any little tucks at the inner corner.

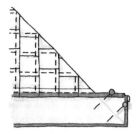

6 Sew by hand or by machine. If machine sewing, set the stitch length to 0 and insert the needle right where the previous stitching ended. Sew a stitch or two before changing to normal length to sew the seam outwards towards the corner. Keep the work well supported to avoid stretching the seam as you sew.

7 Check that the mitre is neat and true before pressing the seam open and trimming any excess fabric. Work all four corners in the same way.

MULTIPLE MITRED BORDERS

If you want multiple borders around the quilt, sew strips of the required fabrics into sets and attach these to the sides of the quilt top. This allows you still to sew only one mitre at each corner, matching up the colours, instead of struggling to sew separate mitres for each round of colour.

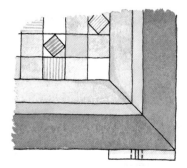

FANCY BORDERS

In this category are designs featuring pieced borders, scalloped edges and appliqué borders. What they have in common is the anxiety they cause about fitting the chosen pattern into a given space. The rule-of-thumb method below, although written for a scalloped edge, will work just as well for dividing up and planning the swags or stems of an appliqué border.

Devising a Scalloped Border

Practise the process in miniature on a small strip of paper. For a rectangular quilt, some initial calculation is required to find a number that divides evenly into both sides so that scallops of the same size appear all around the quilt. To make the calculations easier, you may need to adjust the overall size of the quilt.

1 Decide how many scallops you want on the side of the quilt. Cut a strip of paper as long as the side of the quilt. Fold the strip in half.

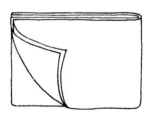

2 Fold in half again. Mark the number of scallop divisions with a concertina-style fold. Unfold half.

3 Using the edge of a plate as a template, mark the curve between the two fold-lines. When choosing the plate size, consider the design of the quilt. It may already have a curved design that you want to echo. Remember that gentle curves will be much easier to sew.

4 Refold the paper but keep the marked scallop where you can see it on the outside. When all the folds are back in place correctly, you should have half of the marked scallop visible as a guide for cutting the curve. If the layers of paper will permit, staple them together before cutting for a more accurate result.

5 Cut along the curve and unfold.

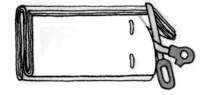

6 Lay the paper pattern on the quilt top and check that the curves are smooth and the correct size. When satisfied, pin the paper pattern to the quilt and mark the outline with basting stitches (see fig. 1).

7 Baste lines at a 45° angle in the corners to help fit the pattern. The outline of the pattern will be the edge of the quilt. This shows you how far to take your quilting design. Do not cut the scallops until you are ready to bind the edges of the quilt top.

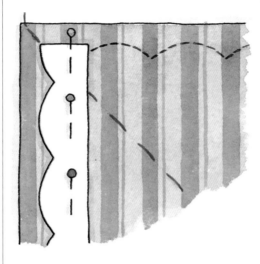

8 Bind with a single narrow 2.5 cm bias binding.

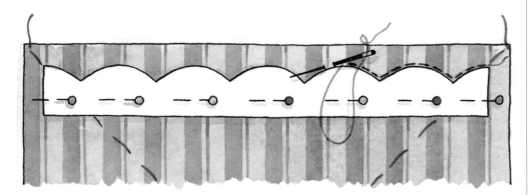

fig. 1

♦ Choose fabrics that are easy to quilt (see page 15).

♦ Beginners are advised to choose small prints to disguise irregularities in quilting.

♦ Do not choose dark backings to put behind light-coloured tops.

♦ The colour of the quilting thread may influence the colour chosen for the backing.

♦ Wash and iron the backing fabric before joining and trimming to size.

♦ Make sure that the backing is larger than the quilt top.

♦ When joining fabric widths, try not to let the seams coincide with the seams on the quilt top.

♦ To avoid a centre seam when two widths are needed to make up the backing, divide one piece equally in two and sew one to each side of the first piece.

♦ If joining selvages, make 1.5–2 cm seams (depending on the actual appearance of the selvage), then trim away before pressing the seam open for less bulk.

♦ Backings can include spare blocks from the front or be assembled from several different pieces of fabric that may continue the theme of the quilt.

♦ The backing can even be a complete design in its own right, making the quilt two-sided.

Binding

....

There are several ways to finish the edges of a quilt. It is your last opportunity to refine your design. Fold-finishing is a traditional and economical method because no extra fabric is needed. Self-binding is quick and easy. The top or the backing must be 2–3 cm larger than the finished quilt to use this method. If the backing is folded to the front, choose a fabric complementary to your design. Separate binding requires more time to complete, but it is versatile and allows the greatest freedom. Double binding uses the most fabric, but it is popular because it makes a firm, durable finish and the folded edge is easy to sew in place.

FOLD-FINISHING

1 Trim the quilt top to the required size plus the turning, the wadding to the finished size, and the backing to the required size plus 1.5 cm turning.

2 Fold both turnings to the inside, enclosing the wadding with the wider one on the backing.

3 Slipstitch the edges together by hand or sew through all layers with a running stitch to match the quilting. Alternatively, machine sew.

SELF-BINDING

1 Trim the top and wadding to the required finished size. Trim the backing as necessary, including a 2–3 cm turning. When 1 cm is turned in, the former finishes to a 1 cm width, the latter to a 2 cm width.

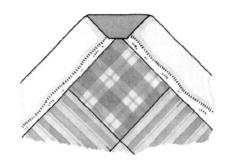

2 Fold the backing to the front, turning in 1 cm, and pin. Make mitres at the corners and baste.

3 Blind-hem in place or machine topstitch. If hand sewing, add a line or two of quilting next to the hemmed edge to keep the wadding from shifting.

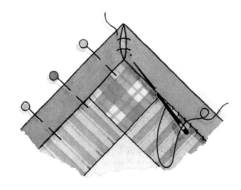

4 To turn the quilt top to the back, reverse the directions.

SINGLE BINDING WITH AUTOMATIC MITRES

1 Before binding, prepare the edges of the quilt by trimming the top so that all edges are straight and even. Using a matching thread, machine or hand stitch a row of running stitches through all the layers within the seam allowance. This will hold the layers securely together and help the binding process. The basting stitches will remain permanently in the quilt. If the binding needs replacing, this task will be easier if the layers are fixed.

2 Beginning along one side of the quilt but not at the corner, place the raw edge of the binding level with the prepared quilt top. Fold over the end as shown and pin the binding to the quilt as far as the first corner.

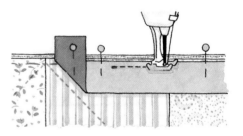

3 Begin stitching 10 cm from the start of the binding. Make sure that the basting stitches are covered by the binding.

4 Stop sewing the width of a seam allowance from the first corner and backstitch a little. Remove your work from the machine (see next page).

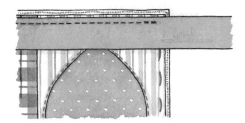

5 Fold the binding up at a 45° angle, then bring it down parallel with the next side to be sewn and level with the raw edges.

6 Pin the binding as far as the next corner and sew it in place.

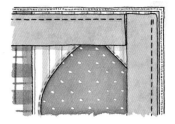

7 Repeat step 5 at each corner. As you approach the beginning of the binding, stop stitching approximately 10 cm away. Backstitch, then remove the work from the machine.

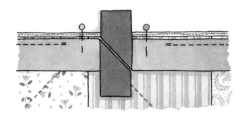

8 For a neat diagonal and join without any overlap ridges, fold the tail of the binding over at right angles to itself and match up with the start of the binding, but in the opposite direction. Where the two folds meet is your seam line.

9 Fold the quilt away from behind the binding, then, with right sides together, machine or hand sew the short diagonal seam.

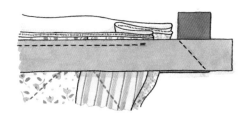

10 Check that the binding fits accurately all the way around the quilt. Make sure that there are no puckers before trimming the excess binding. Finger-press the seam open.

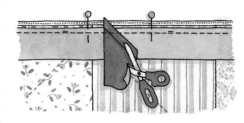

11 With the raw edges of the quilt and binding level, sew the remaining short length of pinned binding to the quilt top. Keep your seam allowance constant to ensure that the two lines of stitching meet in a straight line. Reinforce the join by backstitching at each end.

12 Fold the binding to the back of the quilt. The fullness of the binding at each corner should automatically create neat mitres on the quilt front.

13 On the back of the quilt, fold in the raw edges of the binding and pin in place. Sew to the machine stitching.

14 Slipstitch the mitred folds as you come to them.

DOUBLE BINDING

1 Determine the required finished width of your binding and multiply by six: for example, 0.75 x 6 = 4.5 cm. If working with thick fabrics, such as flannels, add another 0.25–0.75 cm to accommodate the extra thickness. This is the width of strip to cut either on the straight grain or on the bias.

2 Fold the binding in half right side out, and press lightly.

3 As directed for single binding, trim the quilt edges, including the required seam allowance, position the binding with its raw edges to the edge of the quilt, and sew.

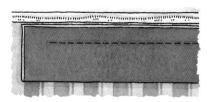

4 Fold the binding to the back of the quilt where the folded edge will be ready to blind-hem to the existing line of stitching.

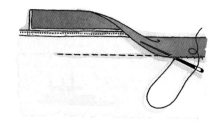

CONTINUOUS BIAS

1 With a rectangle of fabric, right side down (corners must be 90° angles), fold one corner so that the vertical end lines up with the bottom. Press without distorting and cut off the triangle. Repeat at the other end, folding the corner up to the top edge *(see drawing on next page)*.

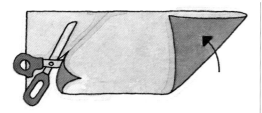

2 On the wrong side of fabric, draw parallel lines the width of the binding required, measuring at right angles from the first diagonal *(shown below)*. Rule 0.75 cm seam lines parallel to the top and bottom edges.

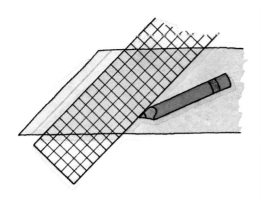

3 Matching point A to point B, as shown above, with a pin inserted through, fold the fabric right sides together. There is a step at the beginning of the seam. Match each line on the top edge with the appropriate one on the bottom edge.

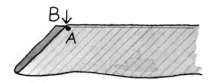

4 Sew along the marked seam with a short stitch length (1.5–2.5 mm). Check that the ruled lines still match before pressing the seam open.

5 Start at point A–B and cut carefully along the ruled lines around the spiral.

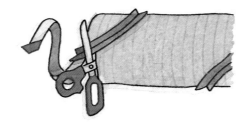

PRAIRIE POINTS

Make singly to use as a decorative feature in a seam. For edging a whole quilt, try the continuous method, which spaces the points evenly.

1 Fold a square in half right side out. Have the fold at the top. Lightly crease the centre vertical.

2 Fold the top-left and top-right corners down to meet at the centre. Crease the diagonals.

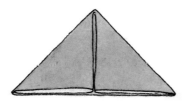

CONTINUOUS PRAIRIE POINTS

1 Determine the size of the finished point and, from that, work out the size of the square needed. Cut a fabric strip twice this width and as long as possible. Fold lengthwise, right sides together. Press and fold open.

2 Divide one half into squares by making a series of cuts as far as the centre fold.

3 On the opposite side, make similar cuts as far as the centre fold, halfway between the ones on the first side.

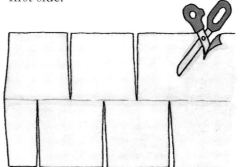

4 With the strip right side down with one long edge to the top, fold each square in turn down to the centre crease, making a fold on the top edge. Then fold the top corners down as for making single prairie points.

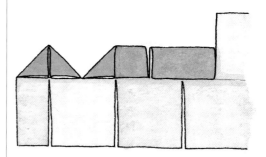

5 When one side is folded, turn and repeat along the second side.

6 Refold the fabric lengthwise to make the continuous points.

7 Sew the continuous points into a seam or insert around the edges of a quilt. Used in this way, the quilt edges need to be fold-finished.

Templates

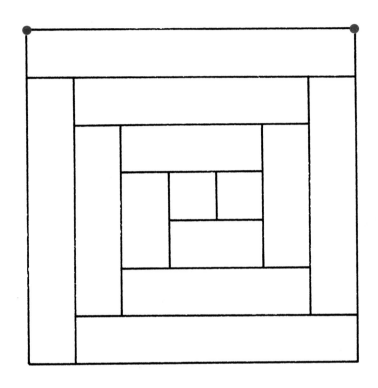

Log Cabin (enlarge to 17.5 cm), p.74

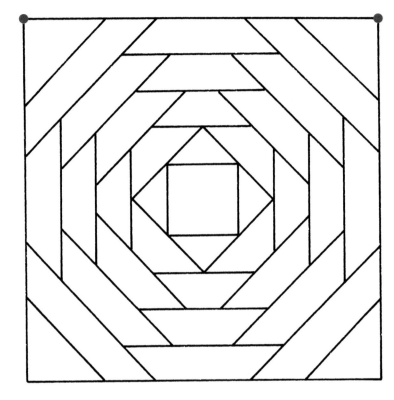

Pineapple Log Cabin (enlarge to 19 cm), p.78

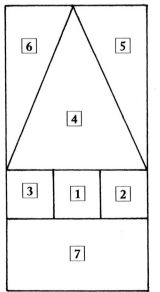

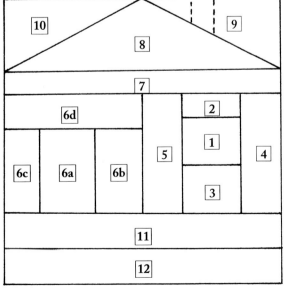

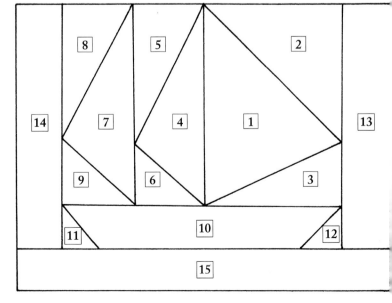

Little Seaside Town Tree (full-size), p.84   *Little Seaside Town* House (full-size), p.84

Little Seaside Town Schooner (full-size), p.84

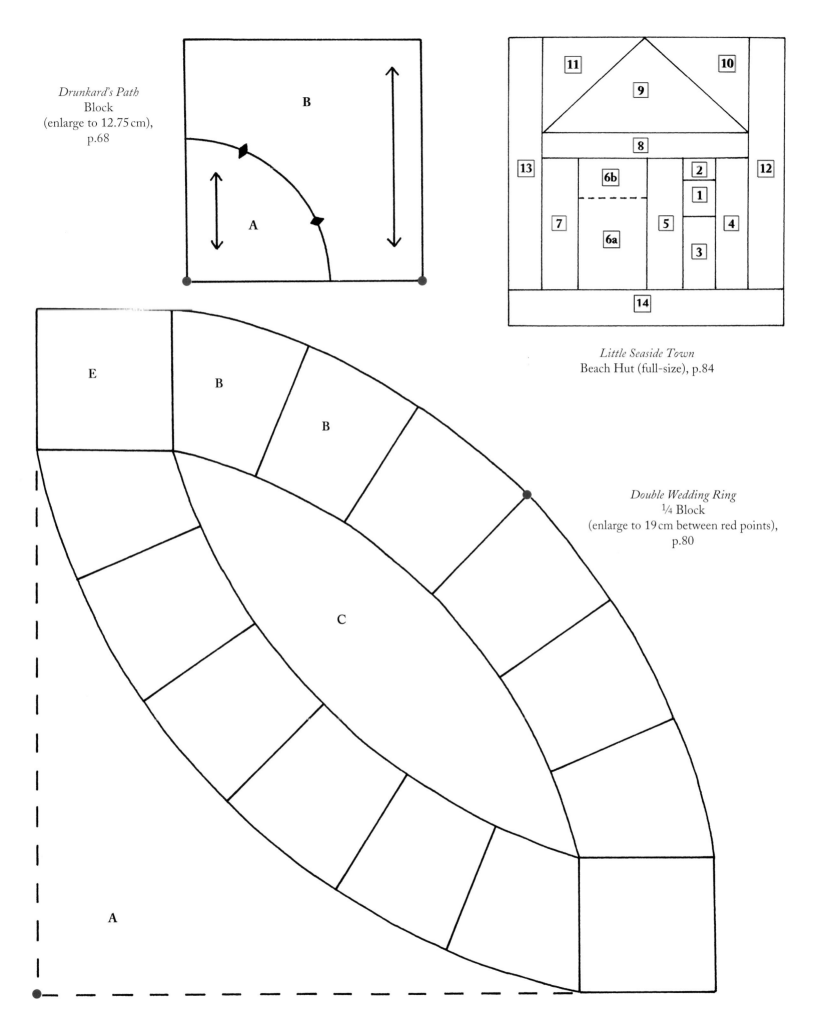

Drunkard's Path
Block
(enlarge to 12.75 cm),
p.68

B

A

| 11 | | | 10 |
9
8
| 13 | | 2 | | 12 |
6b
1
7 | 5 | 4
6a
3
14

Little Seaside Town
Beach Hut (full-size), p.84

E

B

B

C

A

Double Wedding Ring
¼ Block
(enlarge to 19 cm between red points),
p.80

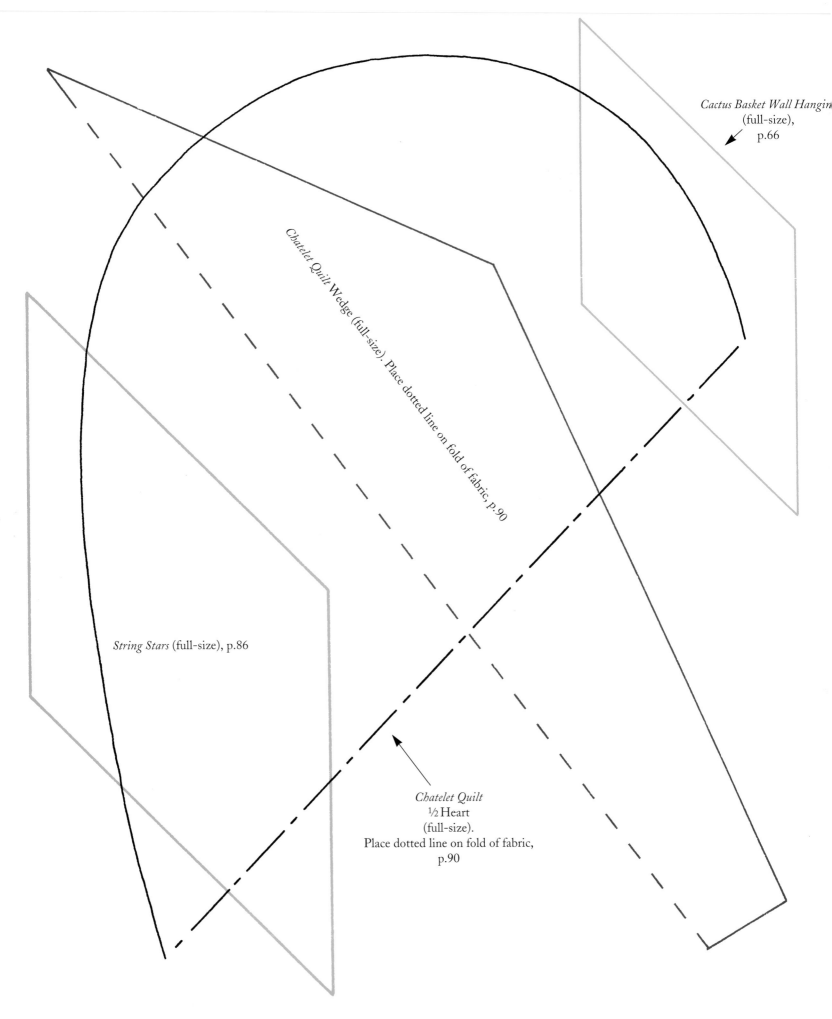

Cactus Basket Wall Hanging (full-size), p.66

Chatelet Quilt Wedge (full-size). Place dotted line on fold of fabric, p.90

String Stars (full-size), p.86

Chatelet Quilt
½ Heart
(full-size).
Place dotted line on fold of fabric,
p.90

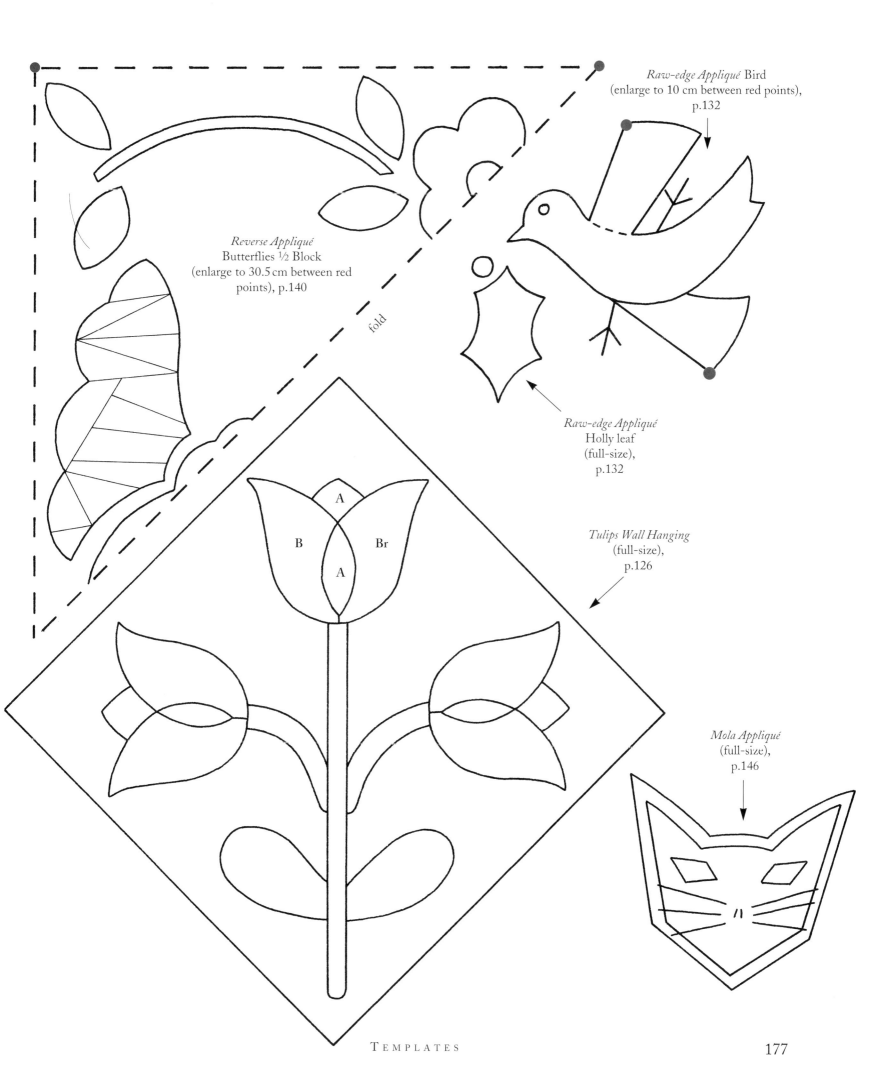

Raw-edge Appliqué Bird
(enlarge to 10 cm between red points),
p.132

Reverse Appliqué
Butterflies ½ Block
(enlarge to 30.5 cm between red
points), p.140

fold

Raw-edge Appliqué
Holly leaf
(full-size),
p.132

A

B   Br

A

Tulips Wall Hanging
(full-size),
p.126

Mola Appliqué
(full-size),
p.146

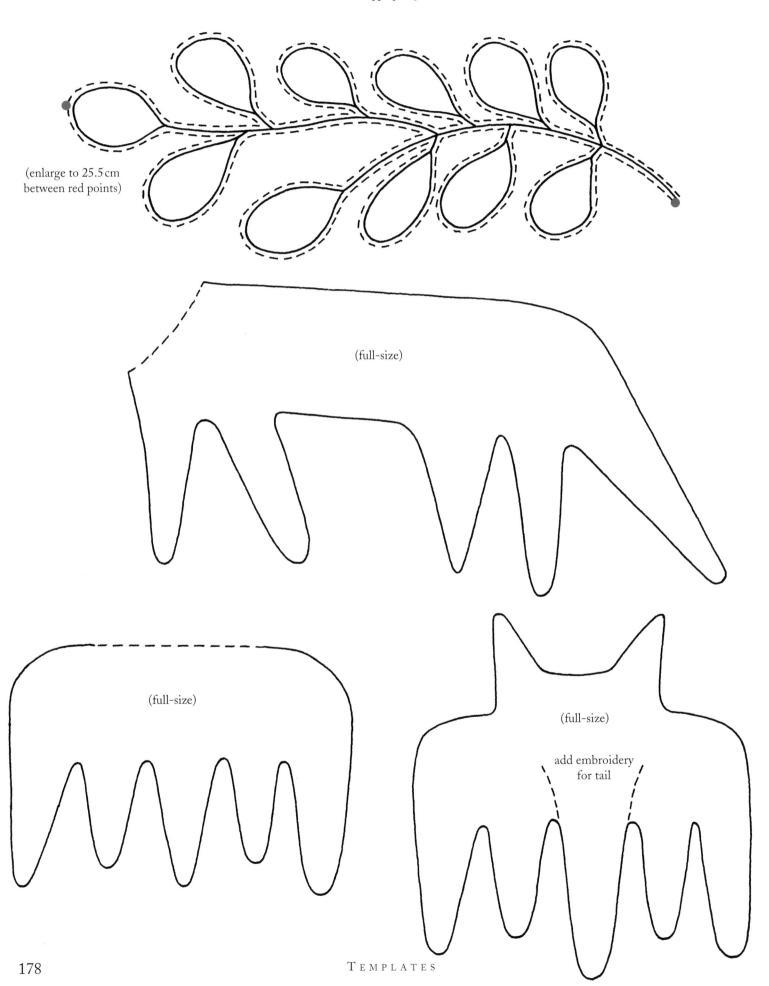

Mola Appliqué, p.146

(enlarge to 25.5 cm between red points)

(full-size)

(full-size)

(full-size)

add embroidery for tail

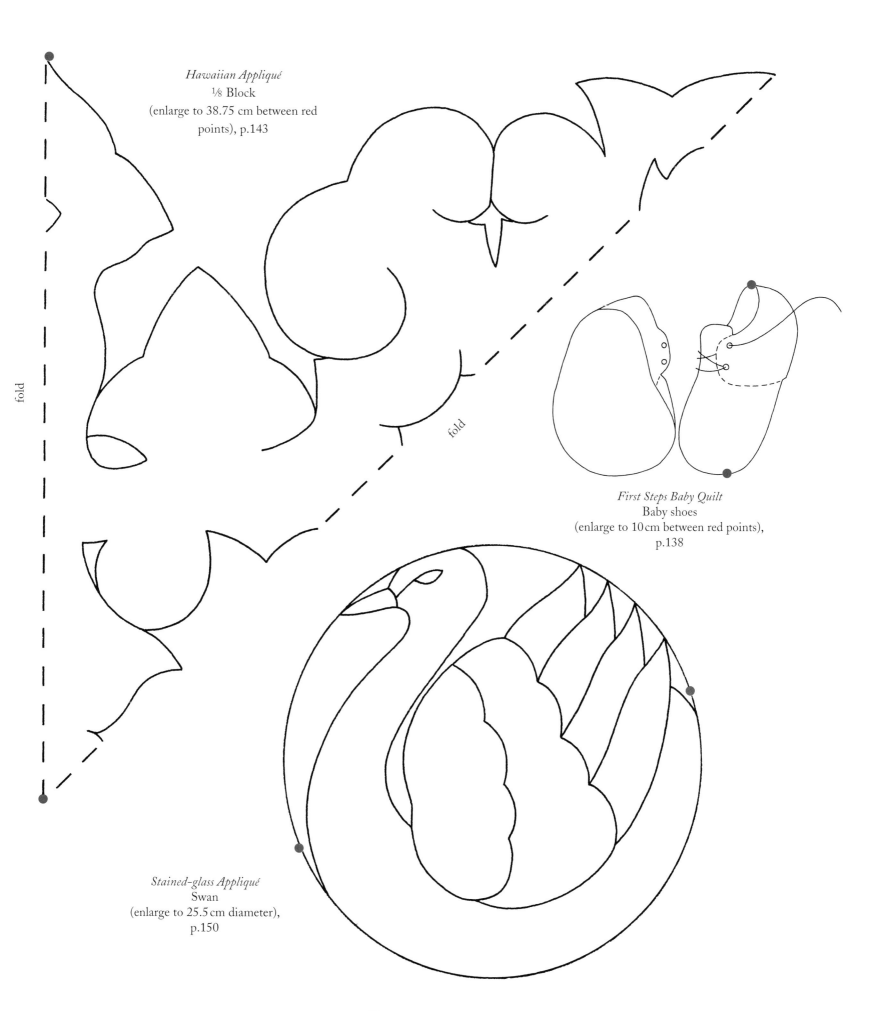

Hawaiian Appliqué
⅛ Block
(enlarge to 38.75 cm between red points), p.143

fold

fold

First Steps Baby Quilt
Baby shoes
(enlarge to 10 cm between red points),
p.138

Stained-glass Appliqué
Swan
(enlarge to 25.5 cm diameter),
p.150

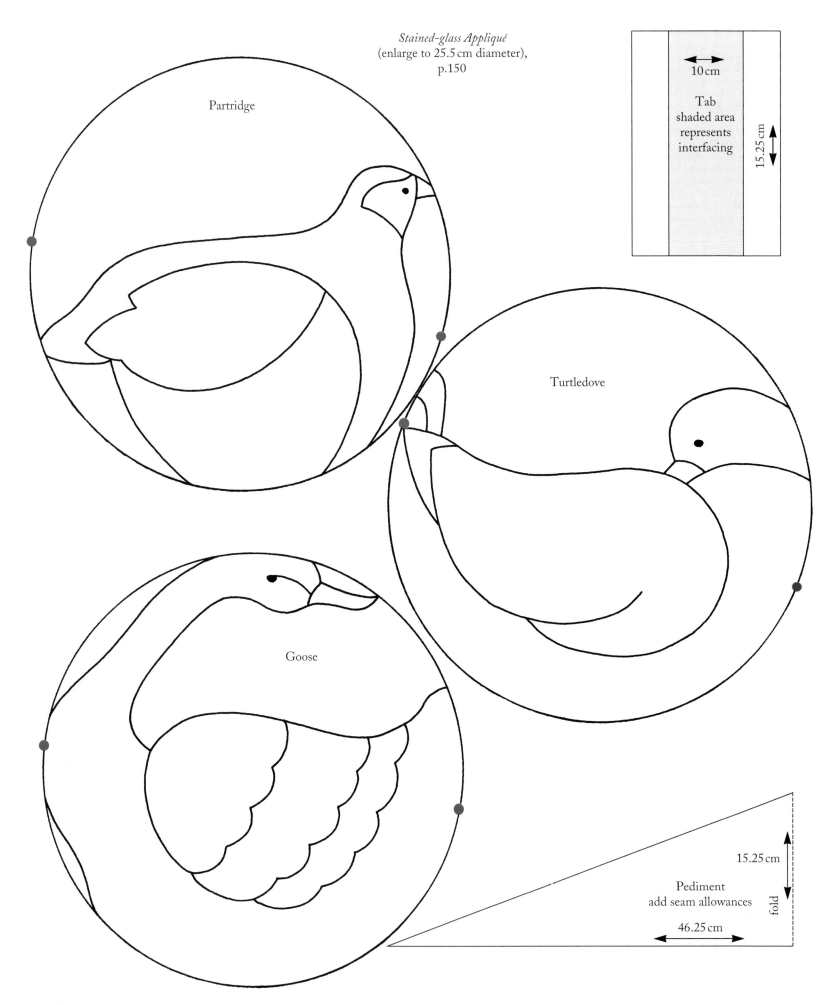

Stained-glass Appliqué
(enlarge to 25.5 cm diameter),
p.150

Partridge

Turtledove

Goose

10 cm

Tab
shaded area
represents
interfacing

15.25 cm

15.25 cm

Pediment
add seam allowances

fold

46.25 cm

Baltimore Basket
Lower left of basket
(enlarge to 9.5 cm between red points),
p.130

Baltimore Basket
Ribbon tails
(full-size),
p.130

Baltimore Basket
Top left of basket
(enlarge to 8.25 cm
between red points),
p.130

Baltimore Basket
Lower right of basket
(enlarge to 5 cm between red
points), p.130

Baltimore Basket
Garland
(enlarge to 26.75 cm between red
points), p.130

Baltimore Basket
Top right of basket
(enlarge to 8 cm between red points),
p.130

Shadow Appliqué
Leaf
(full-size),
p.152

Baltimore Basket
Corner garland
(enlarge to 26.75 cm between red
points), p.130

Baltimore Basket
Bow
(full-size),
p.130

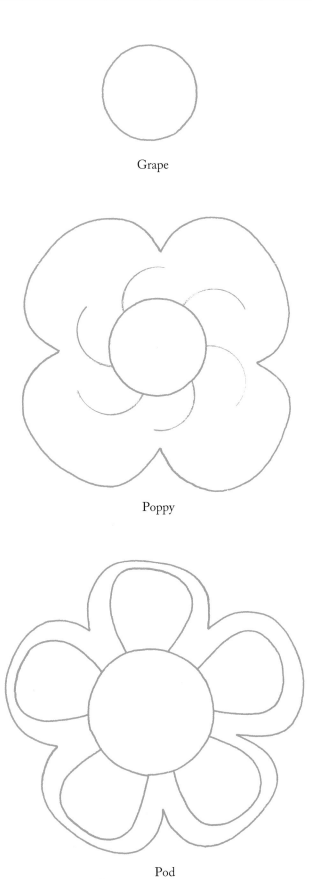

Grape

Poppy

Pod

Baltimore Basket
Ribbon border
(enlarge to 14 cm between red points),
p.130

Shadow Appliqué
Grape, Poppy, Pod
(full-size),
p.152

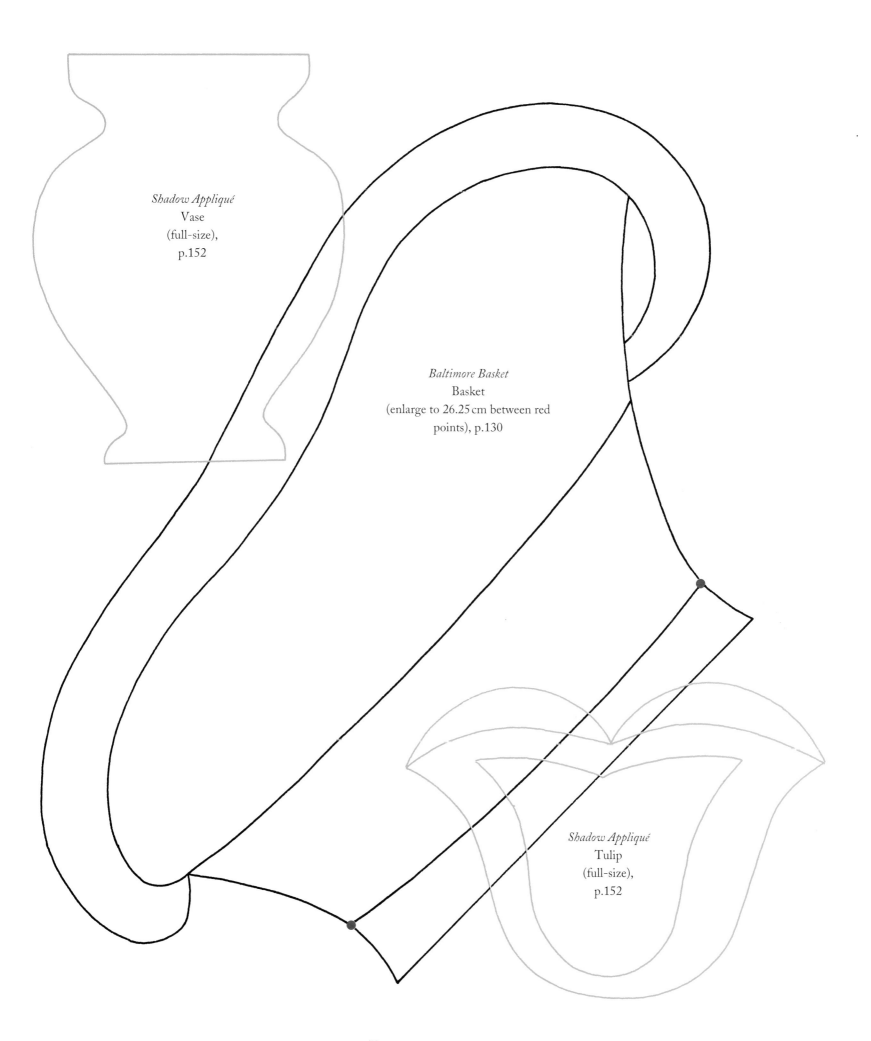

Shadow Appliqué
Vase
(full-size),
p.152

Baltimore Basket
Basket
(enlarge to 26.25 cm between red
points), p.130

Shadow Appliqué
Tulip
(full-size),
p.152

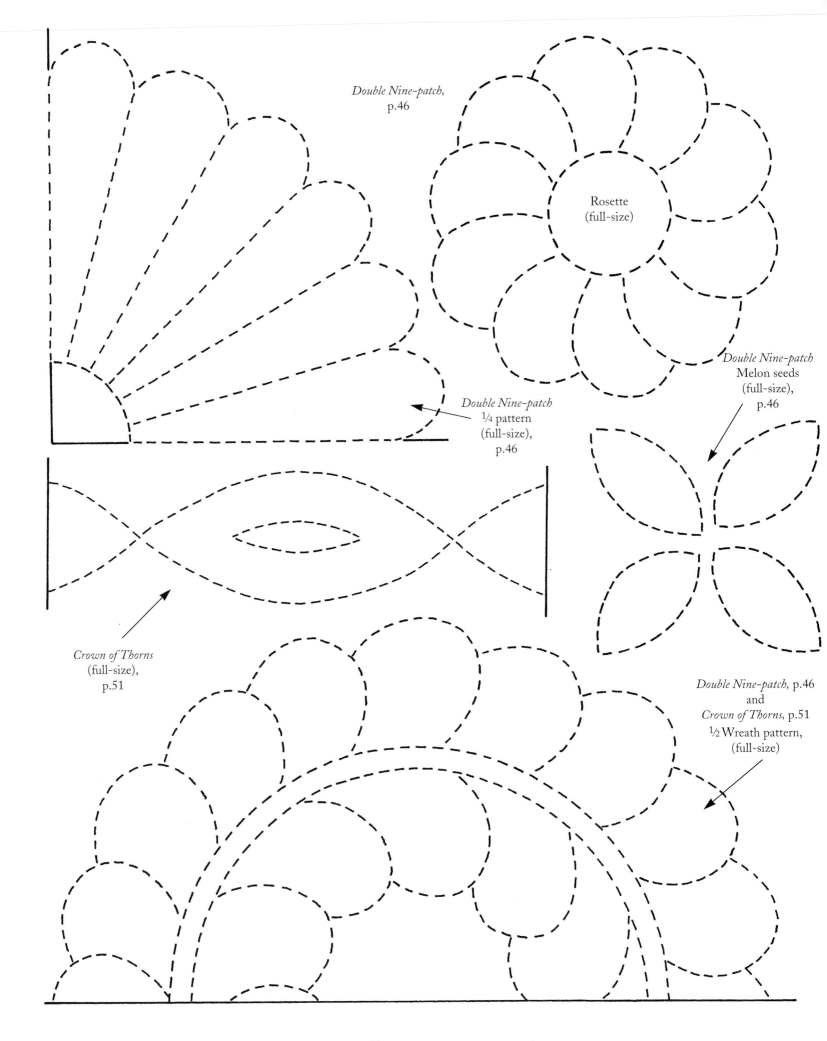

Double Nine-patch,
p.46

Rosette
(full-size)

Double Nine-patch
Melon seeds
(full-size),
p.46

Double Nine-patch
¼ pattern
(full-size),
p.46

Crown of Thorns
(full-size),
p.51

Double Nine-patch, p.46
and
Crown of Thorns, p.51
½ Wreath pattern,
(full-size)

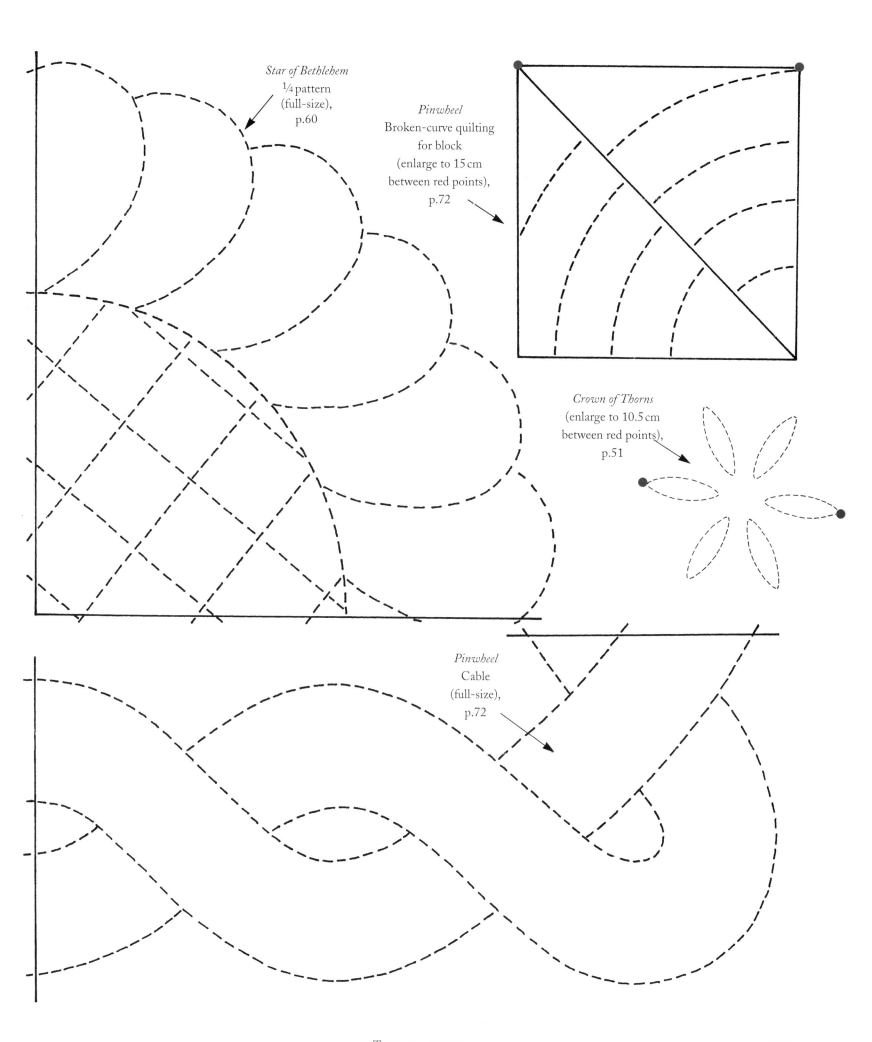

Star of Bethlehem
¼ pattern
(full-size),
p.60

Pinwheel
Broken-curve quilting
for block
(enlarge to 15 cm
between red points),
p.72

Crown of Thorns
(enlarge to 10.5 cm
between red points),
p.51

Pinwheel
Cable
(full-size),
p.72

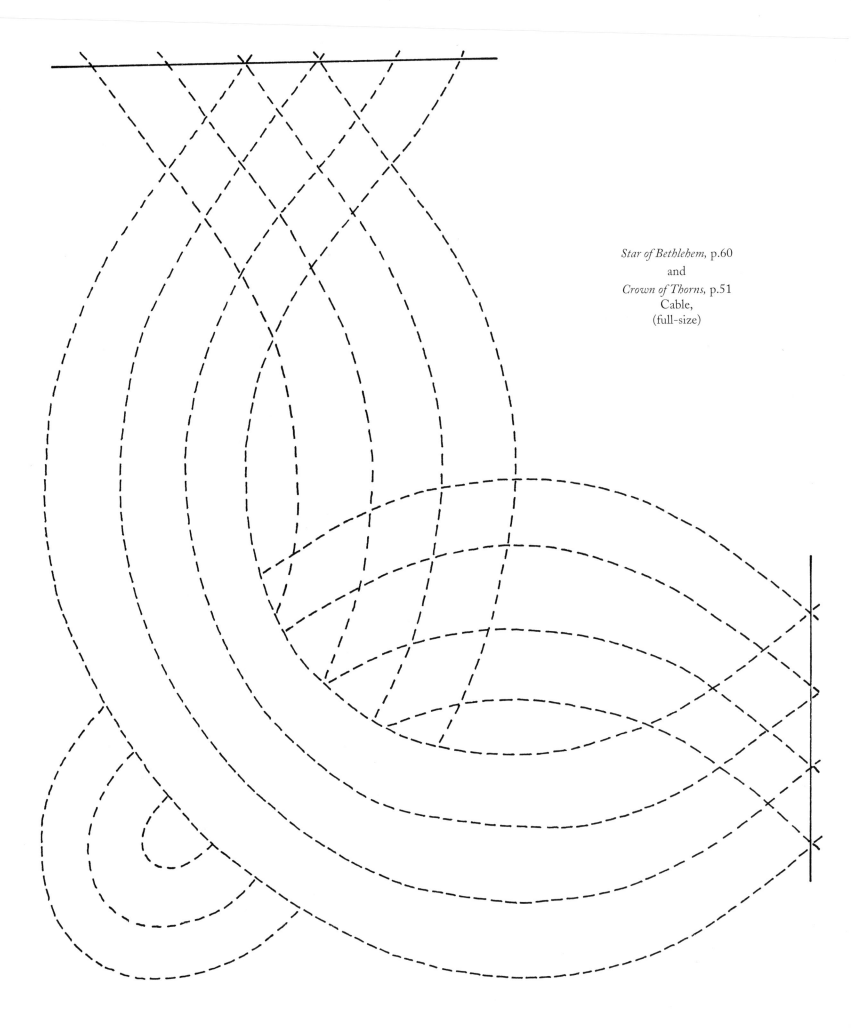

Star of Bethlehem, p.60
and
Crown of Thorns, p.51
Cable,
(full-size)

Hearts and Hourglasses
quilting plan,
p.33

*Black-and-White
Optical-illusion Quilt*
the shaded areas represent
the white-on-white strip-
pieced fabrics,
p.116

Index